Matzo Balls and Christmas Trees

Matzo Balls and Christmas Trees

Memories of My Jewish Mother

Randi Wolf Lauterbach

Printed in the United States.

ISBN: 978-1-9399301-7-0

Library of Congress Control Number: 2013955141

Published by

This book is dedicated to my niece, Alison Walden, and my nephew, Scott Walden, in hopes they will gain an appreciation for some of their grandmother's special qualities.

Prologue

ONE OF MY FAVORITE MEMORIES of my mother is of Christmas Eve, 1964, when I was twelve years old. It was nine o'clock at night, and my mother was talking on the phone to her friend Dora, who lived nearby. Dora was a devout Jewish lady. She observed the Sabbath by attending synagogue regularly, and I believe she maintained a Kosher kitchen. Her son was six years old and was interacting with non-Jewish children and learning about Christmas traditions for the first time. He had asked Dora why Santa Claus didn't visit their home. When my mother hung up the phone, she called me to her. She had a twinkle of inspiration in her eyes as she explained her plan to me. I bought in immediately. We climbed into the family car and drove to the 24-hour Peoples Drug. On the way, I peppered my mother with questions: Would Dora be offended? Would Joey be confused? Mama said, "The child will have a few minutes of excitement at age six. By the time Hanukah rolls around next year, he won't be concerned about Santa Claus. And I think Dora will be thrilled that we did this. As you know, you can't be too offensive with Santa Claus."

When we arrived, the store was very picked-over. This was, after all, Christmas Eve. We did our best to carefully select some gifts suitable for a young boy. I remember buying a keyboard. Then we went home and wrapped the gifts and drove to Dora's apartment. I waited in the car feeling good about our deed as Mama placed the packages on their doorstep with a note "From Santa

Claus." The next morning I joined Mama and Daddy in the kitchen. Mama and I exchanged special smiles. We had some breakfast and finally my sister Sherry joined us. It was a relatively normal morning, and then we all moved into the dining room where the tree was located. One by one, we unwrapped our gifts as we enjoyed another Christmas in our Jewish home.

Our holiday traditions were just one of the ways my mother lived outside the box. Her unique perspective and personality made life interesting for everyone who knew her, but especially for her family. I can't imagine who I might have become without her influence, and I sometimes wonder how my adult life might have differed had she lived long enough to be a part of it.

Margaret Wolf was a complex lady. Born January 29, 1915, the daughter of Orthodox Jewish immigrants, she was a first-generation Jewish-American and lived through much of the history I later studied in school. She learned some difficult life lessons through the proverbial school of hard knocks. Many were learned at an early age. She dropped out of high school in order to work; she helped raise her younger siblings; she fell in love and married outside of her faith; she nurtured her first child during World War II; and she learned about evil and mania by witnessing from afar the persecution of her people during the Holocaust. Her WWII child was Sherry, and I came as her Baby Boomer child eight years later. As if she hadn't had enough *tsuris* (Yiddish for troubles) and responsibility, as her father grew older, she became his primary caretaker. She did so with respect and diligence and personal exhaustion. Clearly, she was very strong and extremely strong-willed.

My sister and I provided her with much enjoyment, and she lived vicariously through us. As a mother, she was doting and protective and involved. She was older than most of my friends' mothers, yet she was always "with it." In today's world, she would have understood pop culture. She always welcomed my friends and always made sure I was hanging out with a good group of kids. Some of my friends found her easy to talk to and visited her when I was absent. She challenged me to do well in school, but with no pressure. That actually made it more difficult because sometimes a good yelling might have inspired me more. Mama never put on any airs, but she did say a couple of times that if you can't be rich, you can at least act it and dress like it! She was witty and engaging. Her wit often helped her get through daily headaches, and she shared her good humor with everyone she knew. Simply put, everyone loved Margaret. She was not self-absorbed in the least. From childhood, she sacrificed her personal time and energy to take care of others: her siblings, her children, her husband, and her father. Given how hard she worked, it was clear why her wishes for Sherry and me included leisure, education, and happiness (and marriage to a rich man).

I lost my mother in December 1974 and my father in January 1975. I was twenty-two and Sherry was thirty. The fact that my mother has been gone for over thirty-five years hasn't diluted my memories. She's not a ghost of the past; she still influences my present. As I travel through life, thoughts of my mother often pop up in the context of the moment. Some small incident will recall to me something she said or did years ago. I caught myself crying recently when I was taste-testing something on the stove. How many times had I watched her do the same thing as she prepared a one-pot meal for family dinner? Often, I'll share humorous anecdotes about her with friends and coworkers, and sometimes I find myself interjecting comments about her as if she were still here and just some distance down the road. I even act out some of her mannerisms. These folks provide a great audience for short stories about Margaret Wolf. And they laugh. And, as my mother would attest, I've always enjoyed an audience.

She handed down to me the notion that the words "I" and "me" are two of the most boring words in the English language. Through the years, I have been very keen at noticing and avoiding people who use those words repetitively in conversation. As a result, I have been reserved in talking about myself. I thought this book might provide a suitable venue for me to finally release *my* thoughts and revelations.

In the fall of 2011, I was travelling with a coworker and sitting shotgun. The fall of the year always makes me a little depressed, as the anniversaries of my parents' deaths approach. I was just thinking about the upcoming holidays that I dread each year, when all of a sudden, I felt as though my brain was going to explode with thoughts of Mama. I pulled out a notepad and began to do what I call a "brain dump." Upon returning home, I took a deep breath and began to review my many notes. I had written them in random order, so it was like putting together a puzzle. None were new thoughts or revelations; I had unveiled most of them through the years, but not in writing. Now I decided to compile them. The timing was significant. I was fifty-nine, the same age my parents were when they died. I wasn't truly superstitious of dying at that age, but somehow the year was calling to me. This was the time to write. Write a book? Why not? I always enjoyed writing, and I could imagine Mama looking down on me and thinking, as she often said, "Randila, you can do whatever you put your mind to."

As you read, you will see how my mother taught me lessons through experiential learning; how she inspired me with positive reinforcement and engagement; how she showed me what a strong woman can accomplish; and most importantly, how she taught me to laugh and laugh at myself.

She also taught me that Judaism comfortably resides in the heart. I do not belong to a synagogue today, but my religion does inspire me. In the news, I pay close attention to Israel. The last time my mother and I went to a synagogue together was in 1972. It wasn't the Sabbath or a holy day. There was an interdenominational service at Beth El, around the corner from our house. It was in memory of the Israelis who had been killed in the Munich Olympics. Those athletes were in our hearts. Some years ago, I considered joining a Synagogue, so I attended services at several of them. I was looking for comfort or enlightenment. At each service, I cried uncontrollably with thoughts of my mother. She wasn't present, but she was there. I didn't find the comfort I wanted, but many years have passed, and I need to try again.

This book is a tribute to my mother—to the unique person she was and to the role she played in my life and the lives of those who knew her. My memories of this astute, intelligent, funny, and strong-willed woman needed to be recorded. My niece, Alison, and nephew, Scott, did not know their grandparents, so this provides some family insight for them. Margaret Wolf was a character, and I offer her character for your reading pleasure.

Chapter 1

Mama and Daddy

I was born on March 7, 1952, in Richmond, Virginia, to Margaret Hyman Wolf and William Harrison "Buck" Wolf. My parents were both thirty-seven and my sister, Sherry, was eight years old. Older moms were not in vogue at the time. I believe my mother was a little tired and decided she'd play it by ear with me. I think she set out simply to enjoy me.

Mama was five feet five inches tall, and a hundred and fifty pounds. Her silvery gray hair in her weekly "do" added about two inches to her height. She had pretty green eyes, but they were obscured by her ever-present eyeglasses. She had lovely skin that I attribute to her Merle Norman cosmetics. She was not beautiful, but she was stunning in her own way.

In her mid-twenties, Mama worked at Thalhimers, a department store in downtown Richmond. She worked in ladies' apparel in the basement, and Buck Wolf worked in shoe repair, also in the basement. I understand he admired her from afar. He chased her for a while and she finally accepted a date with him. She was hesitant because he was not Jewish, and she was self-conscious and unsure of herself. I suppose Daddy's good looks and charm won over both her and her father, because they fell in love and married with a blessing from her dad. Mama became the first and only daughter in her family to marry outside of the faith. My grandfather was much more accepting than my parents expected. With eight children, I suppose he had mellowed a bit through the years.

So there they were around 1942—Mama an Orthodox Jewish lady and Daddy a gentleman who was raised Southern Baptist, ready to meet the world's challenges together. They got an apartment and continued working for Thalhimers. Sherry was born on January 21, 1944. The next year, they moved into my grandfather's house on Hanover Avenue, and that's where they lived when I joined the family.

Mama was the de facto head of the household; she handled the finances, and she raised Sherry and me. Daddy was an onlooker who worked very hard, brought home the paycheck, and never raised his voice to me. He showed more affection than Mama did. I believe my mother was uncomfortable showing affection. When I was a child, the best she could do was give me a kiss on the cheek once in a while. Her demonstrations were generally reserved for when I came running to her with a skinned knee or when I was sick. Those sick days! She'd bring me orange juice, chicken noodle soup, crackers, and a new sick-day toy such as Hi-Q, and I would lie in bed and get treated like a princess.

As for her relationship with my father, I never quite understood it. I think they dearly loved one another, but she was embarrassed when Daddy kissed her in front of me. He teased her a lot, and one of his signs of affection was a pinch on the behind. She'd jump and act offended and embarrassed. He and I would just laugh.

Mama had a presence about her whenever she entered a room—be it a schoolroom, a salon, a ladies boutique, or a bakery. People were immediately drawn to her, and she was well respected. It amazed me how many people addressed her as Mrs. Wolf in public. At home, whenever she decided to sit on the front stoop, within minutes, she attracted neighbors who wanted to visit. She was witty and friendly and someone people wanted to know. She was wise and ready to provide her opinion. She was not afraid to speak her mind. Extroverts obtain their energy from other people and rarely share what's going on with them, and my mother was a quintessential extrovert. She could engage in a conversation for hours with a neighbor or friend, hear all about what was going on with them, and never utter a word about herself. She would interject laughter or jokes whenever the conversation turned to her. She was not one to graciously accept a compliment without coming back with a funny quip about herself. It goes back to the "I" and "me."

Both Sherry and I experienced Mama's overbearing side from time to time. Most notably, she intervened if she didn't approve of our choice in men. At one point in the late '50s and early '60s, she insisted on my sister dating only Jewish boys. "A nice Jewish boy" would grow up to be a doctor or a lawyer or an accountant and make a good living. By the time I came of dating age in the late '60s, she was a bit more open-minded and was probably relieved I was dating respectable boys without regard for religion. But when Sherry and I started contemplating marriage, Mama was almost obsessed with making sure we made the right choices (in her opinion). Although Sherry and I were years apart in age, we both experienced harsh words and arguments with our mother regarding the men who would become our husbands. Mama did not think they could provide adequately for us. She seemed to be okay with her own life, which was without glamour, but she wanted more for her daughters. She just didn't know how to talk to us about her feelings. She could act out, but she couldn't discuss.

Needless to say, we plunged ahead with our relationships despite her efforts to dissuade us. Sherry's marriage has lasted forty-five years; my first marriage lasted two years.

In contrast to my mother, my father was quite an introvert. He worked and he came home. A supervisor of the "line" in a dry cleaners, he oversaw about seventy-five women who handled the cleaning and pressing machines. He was on his feet all day long. His feet would hurt a lot, and he had difficulty finding shoes that were comfortable. I remember he always wore white cotton sox, which seemed to help. His work was exhausting, so when he came home, all he really wanted was a beer, dinner with his family, and a good night's rest.

Daddy enjoyed his beer. His beverage of choice was Richbrau beer, which was brewed in Richmond. He had one each night before dinner. Every other Saturday he'd work a half-day, and afterward he and his buddies would take some time out to drink. When he came home, it would be obvious he'd been drinking. The giveaway was a glassy look in his eyes. Mama and Daddy argued sometimes, and when they did, it was usually one of those Saturdays. Their arguments were quiet and usually occurred in the kitchen. I would sneak downstairs and listen from the other side of the bannister, but I could never figure out what they were saying.

Today, I understand why he wanted to drink. He worked hard, he was raising two daughters, and as time passed, he could look forward to coming home to a demanding father-in-law. Most every night, Daddy retired right after dinner. Because of this, he hardly knew my high school friends or dates, and he didn't participate in school activities. He knew all of my neighborhood friends, as he saw them in the house on the weekends. He was definitely a homebody. On weekends, he sequestered himself in the basement working at his workbench. He fixed clocks on the side. He could fix most anything, and I was sure that one day he would invent something to help people with household tasks. If something was broken, we put it on the workbench and he would work on it when he could. The basement was his retreat.

Daddy was very kind and soft-spoken. I adored him and ran outside to meet him every evening when he came home from work. He would scoop me up, and I would tell him what I had done that day. I believe I was about ten when he suggested a hug might be better than a scoop. I always teased him about school and told him I had received a B on my test or report card, only to show him straight As once he got in the house. Every now and then he would bring me a gift for no particular reason. There was a dime store near his work, and he'd buy my gifts there. To this day, I have a miniature china set he gave me. When I look at pictures of my father today, I realize he was quite handsome.

Daddy had a heart attack when I was fourteen. He was hospitalized for almost a week. I visited him every night with Mama and remember being repulsed by his roommate, who had a terrible cough. Daddy looked fine to me, and I wanted him to come home. I first heard the word "cholesterol" in conjunction with his health. Thereafter, he was on cholesterol medication and on a strict diet. Mama took care of his medications, food, and doctors' appointments.

Knowledge of my father's background is very limited. He was born on April 2, 1915. He also dropped out of high school during the Depression, and his family was poor. He rarely spoke about his family. Periodically while I was growing up, he would take me to visit his mother, who lived outside of Richmond in an area called Glen Allen. His dad died when he was eight years old. His mother remarried, and he never liked her second husband. He had two sisters who lived in Richmond. He visited one often because she was alone and needed some help with groceries. His other sister came to visit us once, and I recall my father being standoffish and my mother carrying on the conversation. I only ever saw my daddy cry three times, and one of those times was when he learned his mother had died.

Chapter 2

The Hyman Family

My mother's father, Henry Hyman, was born in Russia, and her mother, Regina Hyman, was born in Hungary. At the turn of the twentieth century, they independently and proudly made their way through Ellis Island. They both settled in Danville, Virginia, which is where they met. After marrying, they moved to Richmond, Virginia, and opened a grocery store in an area known as Church Hill. Photographs attest to it being a dreary, depressing establishment. They had four sons and four daughters. My mother was the fourth-oldest child and the third-oldest daughter, born January 29, 1915. The family lived upstairs, above the grocery store. The four boys shared one bedroom and the four girls shared another. Their father was overbearing and very strict. My grandmother was quiet and obedient of her husband, which is what one would expect of an immigrant lady at that time. During the Depression, my grandfather requested that several of his children drop out of high school to work. My mother was one of them and dropped out at age fifteen. Other siblings were allowed to complete high school and one actually went on to college. There certainly must have been jealousy among the siblings. The close quarters in which they lived, coupled with a stern father, prevented any outward expression of such emotions, though. They needed to keep the peace, so confrontations were limited.

Through the years, as my grandparents weathered the struggles of their day, they learned English and were thrilled to be in America. They lived in near-poverty but worked hard in the grocery store to overcome it. Henry and Regina practiced Orthodox Judaism, which was not unusual for Jewish immigrants. Thus, they raised their children in this persuasion.

Once their children were grown and out of the nest, my grandparents moved into a house on Hanover Avenue in Richmond. In 1945, shortly after the death of his wife, Grandpa extended an open invitation to any of his children to come live with him. It appeared he was looking for future caregivers. Mama and Daddy's apartment was a few blocks away. World War II was a fact of life and times were tough, so they accepted my grandfather's offer. My father loved to tell us what Grandpa said to him when they moved in. In his thick accent, he said, "Velcome, Buck. Please no pictures of Jesus on the vall."

My mother's brother Larry served in WWII. Upon his return, there was a grand homecoming at the house that some of the neighbors remember to this day. There were banners hanging on the porch and a big party! And now that Larry was finally safe at home, the Hyman family was in a position to relax and enjoy peacetime.

After the war, the family had some wonderful gatherings on Hanover Avenue. On Saturday nights, my mother's brothers, sisters, in-laws, and their children would converge on the house. Grandpa had a special "music machine" with a microphone built into it. They would sing into the microphone and the machine would cut records! They sang and danced and enjoyed each other. For accompaniment, Grandpa played the mandolin and my mother's sister played the piano. Grandpa made some whiskey called

Vishnick and he would share it at family gatherings. He kept it in his closet, and somehow Sherry got into it when she was six or seven. Luckily it tasted so bad she didn't drink a lot. Regurgitation quickly helped to rid her body of it.

One of the eldest grandchildren, my sister was put on a pedestal by the entire family. Everyone adored Sherry. She remembers some of the Hyman gatherings. Unfortunately for me, I missed most of the post-World War II fun times. Somewhere along the way, feuds erupted and the family began to fall apart. This sister didn't speak to that brother; this sister-in-law didn't speak to that sister. It was the Hyman family soap opera. By the time I was old enough to remember, I just saw the occasional aunt or uncle and some cousins. Mama never explained the feuds. I wasn't there for the fun, but at least I inherited the Hyman interest in music and dancing.

Of course, living with my grandfather, I saw lots of him growing up. He was a proud immigrant who spoke broken English, but at least it was English. I loved to listen to him talk. I remember he would sit on the front porch as I ran up and down the sidewalk doing whatever you do when you run up and down the sidewalk. Every now and then as I passed our house, I would hear Grandpa yell: "Randila, slow down! You're gonna fell down! You're gonna fell down!"

Grandpa learned tailoring at some point in his life. He transitioned from grocer to tailor and had a tailor shop on the other side of town. "H. Hyman Tailor" was the inscription above his door. He had his car and he drove to and from the shop every day. One day he came home with a cut above his eye. Mama asked, "Papa, what happened?" "I don't know. I velt a little bump on the bridge." Well, the passenger side of the car was pretty well messed up. Daddy drove to the Lee Bridge and when he got back, he reported that half of the car was on the bridge!

It wasn't long after this that my mother began taking Grandpa to and from work every day. I rode with her to pick him up each afternoon. I loved playing with the tailor chalk they used in the shop. He had two ladies working with him and they always let me "explore."

Grandpa's shop was a block from the city courthouse, and he was reputed to know every judge and lawyer in town. I assume many of them were his customers. He also knew every street person on Hull Street. I had the distinguished opportunity to meet some of those street people while spending time with my grandfather. Every Christmas, Mama would brace herself when it was time to pick up Grandpa. It must have been exhausting for Grandpa to drink with every street person, every lawyer, and every judge in town. He served Vishnick to his friends. The first time I heard the expression "poured him into the car," I knew Grandpa was drunk. Merry Christmas from the Jewish Russian Immigrant! He gave me a bicycle one Christmas (and yes, it was for Christmas!). I loved the bike, except for the fact that it had a nameplate on it that read "Randy" instead of Randi. It was okay because it came from him. Grandpa also gave me silver dollars every now and then. I still have every one of them.

When I was ten or so, Grandpa was diagnosed with hardening of the arteries. Soon after, Mama and Daddy convinced Grandpa it was time to retire. He had delivered a suit with one sleeve eight inches shorter than the other. Grandpa retired, slowly went downhill, and was extremely demanding of my mother and father as his caretakers. My parents weathered his aging years with their own exhaustion. He had a bell in his room and would ring it when he wanted something. Mama was up and down those steps multiple times a day. Bathing him was an ordeal for my father. Finally, when they were beyond their limits, Grandpa went into a nursing home. He died one week later. I was twelve.

It was extremely hot the day of his funeral, and the gravesite was on a rather steep hill. I fainted in the middle of the service. I woke up in someone's car that had air conditioning. Apparently the cantor had been singing when I fainted. He put his head through the window, looked down at me, and asked if his singing was that bad. Grandpa must have been thinking, "Randila, it's hot. You're gonna fell down!"

Mama had seven siblings; one died very young. So I knew four uncles and two aunts and their spouses. There were fifteen cousins. Mama was sort of the hub of the family. She kept in touch with most of her siblings. The three I knew best were Uncle Herman, Aunt Rose, and Uncle Virgil.

Uncle Herman was married to Aunt Fage and was widowed relatively young. He visited every Sunday precisely at two o'clock for dinner. At precisely 1:45 every Sunday, Mama would yell, "Someone make sure the door is unlocked!" If it was locked, Uncle Herman would practically pull down the door trying to open it. He was brainy and not mechanical. He was a very generous uncle. He took my sister and me on clothes shopping sprees the likes of which I've not experienced since. This was his way of thanking Mama for making him part of our family.

Uncle Herman lived in a nice high-rise apartment in downtown Richmond. As expected, the women outnumbered the men. I'm sure he was considered a great catch among the widows. Every Sunday, Uncle Herman's dinner conversation contribution was a weekly recounting of his latest dates. He would tell us all about the ladies and what he liked and didn't like about each one. Unbeknownst to him, I began to keep a journal of his comments, and, of course, Mama loved reading them. Her favorite was "She was a very nice lady; very intelligent and attractive, but she had a slight B.O." I never showed the journal to Herman and it's long since gone.

Herman sometimes took me to visit his brother Sonny. He and his wife, Doris, had six children. I played with two of them during our visits. My favorite was my cousin Jeanna. She had Down syndrome and was very sweet and pleasant to be with. She shared her toys with me and was interested in my being there.

Herman was a bookkeeper and had been with his company for many years. As was true of most of the Hyman family, Uncle Herman enjoyed gambling. I befriended a former FBI agent years after Herman passed away. I'm not sure how we got on the subject, but this agent had been on Herman detail due to the fact that he had been one of the biggest bookies in Richmond. I was so proud to hear! Bookkeeper—bookie . . . makes sense.

My mother's sister Rose lived in Maryland and would take the train to visit us about twice a year. A typical visit was an event for me. I loved going to Broad Street Train Station to pick her up. She would stay for three or four days. Aunt Rose would take it upon herself to rearrange the kitchen or try to organize something in the house during each visit. This aggravated Mama. Rose drank "real" coffee, and my mother was the poster child for anything instant. So just to test Rose, one time she made instant coffee, put it in the percolator, and offered it to her sister as if it were percolated coffee. Rose knew immediately. Rose always let me play with her makeup. She wore a wig, but that was off-limits for dress-up. She and Mama were close friends, and all in all, the visits were fun for both of them, though by the end of Rose's stay, Mama was always happy to make that drive back to the train station to wave goodbye to her sister. At the same time, she looked forward to her next visit.

Uncle Virgil was one of Mama's younger brothers. He and his wife, Glen, lived in Richmond. I thought he could have been the next Johnny Carson. He always had something funny to say, and he was interested in what other people had to say. Virgil and my father were good friends. When the two of them got together, it was usually for cookouts and drinking beer—the simple life. My sister married when I was fifteen, and after that, my brother-in-law, Gene, was taken into their tutelage on several occasions. They told Gene they were going to teach him how to fish . . . the right way. So they went fishing. This is how the fishing trips went: They would get to the pier, throw their lines in, and go directly to the restaurant for a "couple of beers." Periodically one of the three would go outside to check the lines to see if any mammoth fish had swum into the hook and caught itself. The day progressed and it was time to go home—without any fish and with a few beers under their belts. One time they stopped at a fish market in downtown Richmond, bought some fish, and tried to pass them off to Mama and Glen as the catch of the day. The white wrapping paper may have given them away.

Chapter 3

Early Memories

My family lived in an area of Richmond referred to as the Near West End, a short distance from Robert E. Lee Elementary, Albert H. Hill Junior High, and Thomas Jefferson High School, all excellent neighborhood schools. Our house was an unconnected row house probably built in the 1930s. The front porch often served as a playroom for games and dolls and gatherings with the neighborhood kids. The living room had a combination of furnishings: a recliner for Daddy and Grandpa, a sofa upon which I would stand and peer out the window to see what was going on outdoors, chairs, tables, and an upright piano. A fireplace was lit once in a while, and I learned the significance of the flue when it wasn't opened a couple of times. The dining room had a lovely dining set, which included a large dining table, my grandmother's china cabinet, and a buffet. The buffet drawers were full of anything you could imagine: music albums, wrapping paper, pens, paper, candles, doilies. Radiators warmed the rooms in the winter; and for hot, humid summers, one air conditioning unit in the dining room window cooled the downstairs.

The kitchen was a decent size, with a gas stove and a fridge with the freezer on the bottom. There was no dishwasher. Mama was the dishwasher, with occasional help from Sherry. I can remember Mama standing at the sink with a cigarette hanging from the corner of her mouth. We had a Formica table and upholstered chairs and we gathered for family dinners.

There was a small room between the living room and the kitchen that we called the telephone room. In that room was a desk with a phone and sometimes a manual typewriter, a secretary, and bookshelves full of books. From there you could go to the basement. It was a full basement, and it was my father's haven. A huge, round, oak table was a catch-all surface for whatever you wanted to place in the basement. From his workbench, Daddy taught me how to use many of his tools. To this day, I sometimes amaze myself when I'm able to fix things around the house. The washer was down there, and there was no dryer. A refrigerator was usually stocked with drinks and beer. There was a sole commode in its own "water closet." The exterior door went to the backyard, where the clothesline was located.

The backyard was of a typical size for a city yard. A narrow cement walkway ran the length of the yard. At the end of the walkway was a tree with berries. We never knew what kind of berries they were, but the kids and I ate them every year. The trash cans were next to the tree. Mama planted bulbs on a little patch between the walkway and the fence. She also had some perennial bushes. The prettiest forsythia bush graced the end of the yard. Next to the porch was a patch of mint that grew and grew, and we used it in our iced tea. Our yard was the setting for many kids' activities through the years.

Of course, the staircase was in the living room. Upstairs there was one full bathroom, three bedrooms, and a sleeping porch. For comfortable sleeping, Daddy had exhaust fans placed in select windows. When they blew out, cool air flowed into other windows in the house. We never had a sleepless night due to heat.

The sleeping porch was probably the most interesting room in the house, as it had windows on three walls. Sleeping arrangements were ever changing. When I was a little girl, Grandpa slept in the larger front room, Sherry in the smaller front room, Daddy on the sleeping porch, and Mama and me in the middle room. Eventually I migrated to the small room and finally the big front room, after Grandpa died and Sherry got married.

When I was a baby, Sherry was taking care of me one day in the sleeping porch. She placed me on the bed. I rolled off and under the bed and she was screaming out the window to Mama, who was putting clothes on the line: "Randi's dead! Randi's dead!" Obviously I was okay! She always says she liked having me around. As I got older and nosier, I enjoyed going to her room, and she would let me look at all of her "stuff." She hugged me all the time and liked to pick me up. I was like one of her dolls. She says she was never jealous of me.

My mother did not work when I was in elementary school. She was always there. "Eat your breakfast, Randi. You need to fill that cavity in your stomach." "Come inside and rest for a while." "What do you want for lunch?" "More milk? I should buy a cow for the backyard." "Invite your friends in for lunch." "You look cute in that outfit." So it's not surprising that when it was time for me to start school, the adjustment was difficult for both of us.

In 1957 I began attending junior primary, which is what my school called kindergarten. To say that the apron string followed me all the way to school would be quite an understatement. I cried every day. For the first few weeks of school, Mama drove me. I should say she drove us. Not only was she at the school for the first several weeks of kindergarten, she stood outside of my classroom and periodically waved to me through the window in the door.

Yes, I sat in the classroom and looked out to see my mother every now and then to make sure she was there. Finally, my teacher, Miss Carter, suggested my mother go home. We both survived.

I had a fabulous childhood, but a few things make me wonder how my generation made it through the sixth grade. In kindergarten, air-raid drills were exciting elements of some school days. The alarm would sound, and for reasons we never quite understood, we would line up in an organized fashion and go into the basement of the school. Then we stooped down to hug ourselves while balancing against the wall. Finally, we'd get back in line and return to our classroom, as though the diversion were as much a part of our curriculum as the three Rs. It's amazing that all Baby Boomers today don't just drop down whenever they hear sirens. I asked Mama about the drills and she candy-coated it and told me that they were good exercise, and she might start having them at home! I worried about things that most kids didn't, and therefore was a little high-strung. Somewhere along the line I learned about bombs, because when I found out Mama and Daddy weren't going to build an air-raid shelter in the backyard, I broke down, wailing, "How could you let us die like that?"

Then there were the polio vaccines that were administered to students on sugar cubes. For some reason going to school on a Saturday to eat a sugar cube for health purposes seemed silly to me. What was my doctor for? And they wondered why I had occasional grey hairs as a child?

We had "show and tell," as did every other kindergarten class in the nation. My mother liked history and had a collection of old newspapers with historic headlines. She also had some ration stamps from World War II. While kids typically brought in toys for show and tell, I brought in ration stamps one day. My classmates learned that my mother had to use the stamps to buy milk for my sister when she was a baby. But it didn't stop there. I was actually able to explain blackout curtains too! The kids were enthralled, I'm sure. It's interesting to reflect that a short thirteen years prior, those headlines and ration stamps weren't history for my family; they were just a fact of life.

I could never open the milk cartons at school. It was a source of stress for me every day. Finally I told my mother, and she bought me a thermos. She put V8 in the thermos because I loved it. The kids at lunch teased me and said I was drinking blood. But what really bothered me was that for some reason, I couldn't hold onto a thermos. I must have broken three of them in one school year. Mama was very patient with me, and then came summer.

In the summers I would stay busy with the other kids. But if there was a period of no activity, I would aggravate my mother: "There's nothing to do." "Go watch television." "There's nothing on." "What do you mean there's nothing on? There's always something on the TV." "What can I do?" "Go find one of your friends." "They're not at home." "Go iron some sheets or pillowcases. Practice the piano. If you don't leave me alone, I'm going to smack you on the tuchas. Go outside and get some sun." I'd go upstairs and take a nap or play with makeup or figure out how next to bother Mama.

One blessing for her was the set of tickets we all had for the Byrd Theater. Each year at the end of the school year you could buy a series of summer tickets for this theater on Cary Street. Built in 1928, the Byrd Theater is a beautifully maintained building that's still in operation today, albeit slightly worse for wear than when I visited it as a child. Inside is a huge chandelier, upholstered seats, and a wonderful balcony, which is where we kids usually congregated. Before the movie, the stage in front of the screen would open up, and a Wurlitzer organ would miraculously rise into view, organist and all. He would play songs while you waited for the movie to begin, and then descend below the stage as magically as he'd appeared. We probably couldn't tell you which movies we watched there. It was more of a social time. I do recall that most of the movies were animated. We went once a week throughout the summer, and the gang would *walk* to Cary Street without fear for our lives. The walk was fun, and it was just something simple that we enjoyed. Even in those days, we were conscientious about our money. Before going to the theater, we would stop at the Peoples Drug store to buy our candy because it was cheaper there.

Living in the South, we had the usual summer storms with the much-anticipated lightning and thunder and winds. There was heat lightning and regular lightning. Heat lightning offered you a chance to calculate how far away the storm was. Lightning would strike without a sound. After the heat lightning you could count slowly, and when the thunder eventually crashed, your count represented the distance to the storm in miles. Regular lightning usually crashed with thunder simultaneously. And it was close. Yes, we were meteorologists early on. A beautiful maple tree in front of our house was our indicator of how fast the winds were blowing. We never experienced a tornado, but I recall thinking of *The Wizard of Oz* when the winds got high.

I was a nervous wreck during those storms. I worried that lightning would strike the tree and then the house. But the worst thing about the storms was that my mother and sister would sit on the porch on the *metal glider* and watch the excitement. I was usually inside on the couch, yelling out the window, "You're going to get electrocuted! You need to come inside!" They would just turn around and wave. It was a type of abuse, I do believe.

During the winter, it was harder to keep me occupied. Whenever it snowed, I'm certain Mama saw it as a chance to get me out of her hair and allow her to have some alone time. She would bundle me up and shove me through the door to "go play and enjoy yourself." I'd come back in, complaining that it was too cold or too wet or too uncomfortable out there. And sure enough, she was equipped. She'd have another pair of gloves, another scarf, and another hat warming on the radiator. She'd give me the requisite milk that I loved and shove me back through the door. A few minutes later I'd come back in thirsty or hungry. "What about the sled? Have you used the sled?" No, because I was afraid I'd fall off. "What are the other kids doing?" "I don't know . . . snowball fights." I was a nag, let's face it. The Yiddish term is "nudnick." I believe if you were to look that word up in a Yiddish dictionary, you would have seen my little face.

Barbie dolls, jacks, pickup sticks, drawing, and pestering Mama were my main pastimes early on. She made some Barbie clothes, which I treasured because they were different from all the rest. She was the absolute best audience for my antics. I would cross my eyes and tell her they were stuck. I'd come downstairs with white powder on my face and tell her I didn't feel well. She used Merle Norman cosmetics. I would play with them. I would put on one particular red masque and appear before her in an effort to scare her. She always faked it. Overall, she would just laugh and laugh at me. I was a smart kid with a sense of humor. And she simply enjoyed me.

We didn't have many pets growing up. I remember having goldfish and, at one time, a duck. No, we didn't have dogs or cats like most families. We had goldfish and a duck. The goldfish were the cause of many arguments between Mama and me. Who wanted to clean out that nasty bowl? Certainly not *me.* But when I saw that cigarette hanging out of the corner of Mama's mouth, I knew it was my turn, no ifs, ands, or buts.

And the duck! Who in the world decided to buy a duck? To this day I do not know. That duck followed Mama around constantly. She would go outside to hang clothes on the line and the duck was underfoot. Inside the house, the duck was an appendage of hers. One day, we took the duck to Byrd Park Lake. My parents said this would be a better place for him. But our duck was yellow and the others were white. That bothered me. Not to worry, they assured me. Almost immediately after arriving at the lake, my father started talking to a young man. The next thing I knew, the man took the duck and its food and walked away. Bye-bye, duck. I must say I didn't lose a lot of sleep over that duck.

In her teenage years when she began to drive, my sister, Sherry, took me everywhere with her. I was eight going on sixteen. There was practically a generation gap between us, but we had fun together. To this day I wonder if my mother paid her to take me off of her hands for a while.

Sherry actually took me places with her friends. I went to high school sorority meetings with them. In my eight-year-old mind, I was a member of the group. I did aggravate her, don't get me wrong. At one point, her grades were slipping and Mama thought it was because she talked on the phone too much. Mama tasked me with hiding her phone. I loved watching her look frantically all over the house. I finally fessed up that it was in the clothes hamper.

When she finished high school, she went to work. Each day she left before I left for school. I would sneak her clothes, wear them to school, and replace them before she got home. I was the only kid in the fifth grade wearing Villager sweaters and ascots, which were in style at the time. Mama tried to special-order a pair of Weejuns for me because those were the "cool" shoes. They didn't make them in a size three.

I was in awe of my big sister. In our tween years, she took my friends and me to the beach for the day; she took us to the state fair; and she would drive us to the local hamburger joint. She pampered me.

Once she settled into her job, she decided to pay me an allowance. She was paid every two weeks, and on her payday, I received twenty-five cents. For that twenty-five cents I would do "stuff" for her. I'd fix her a sandwich, get her a glass of milk, run upstairs to fetch her shoes, go to the basement for this or that . . . on and on. I was running all over the house for my allowance. Daddy pulled me aside one day and said, "I want you to do the math with me. Sherry is paying you twelve and half cents a week to run, run, and run." We discontinued the allowance.

My mother taught me to stand up for what is right at an early age. When I was nine, some friends and I purchased some mini-foods to play with with our Barbies. There were fruits and vegetables, breads, meat—everything you could want. They came through mail order. Well, one day I noticed my friend had a few pieces that I didn't have. I actually compared her mini-foods with mine, one by one. When I determined what was missing from my box, I told Mama. She handed me a piece of paper and the address on the side of the box. She told me to write a letter of complaint. I did just that. About a week later I received two whole boxes of mini-foods with an apology letter. That paid off!

In the fifth grade, a boy did karate chops on my head whenever I bent over to get water out of the water fountain on the play yard.

Living in the city, we were fortunate enough to actually—now get this—walk to school. One day I had just arrived home after school when there was a knock on the door. It was HIM! He'd followed me home! I slammed the door in his face. Mama was right behind me, and I had to explain. She scolded me, saying how rude it was regardless of what a pest he had been. I'll never forget these final words: "He likes you, Randila!" That was my first lesson in how boys show they "like" you. And I do remember her chuckling later when relaying it to Daddy. Margaret Wolf, Etiquette Advisor.

(By the way, part of being Jewish is to understand that any name can be modified into a Jewish pet name by simply adding -ala or -ila to the end of the word. Thus, Randila is a pet name for Randi.)

In the sixth grade I received a C in geography on my six-week report card. I was very upset. I had always been a straight-A student. Well, my mother was very active in the school and the PTA, and when she visited the geography teacher to find out what the problem was, it seemed to have a miraculous effect on my progress. I received an A for the next six weeks. Margaret Wolf, Teaching Advisor.

It was during recess in the sixth grade that I learned President Kennedy had been assassinated. It was a weird day for an eleven-year-old. Mama was very upset when I got home. I had a piano lesson and we decided to go. When we arrived, people were cancelling their lessons. My teacher cried during the lesson. My parents were very quiet that evening watching Walter Cronkite, who also cried.

Once in a while, Mama would wake me up and suggest I needed a day off from school. We would go out for breakfast at Peoples Drug on Cary Street. That was so much fun. I always got toast with jam. For some reason, toast and jam was special when I was out with my mother and playing hooky from school. And we always held hands as we strolled and said we were girlfriends. Margaret Wolf, Truancy Pusher.

Mama often shopped at Giant Food in the Willow Lawn Shopping Center because they had "real" delicatessen food. After the kid loaded the groceries in the car and my mother handed him the requisite tip (sometimes she let me hand him the tip) she would search through the groceries. I always knew what she was doing and waited eagerly. She'd pull out the pastrami or the corned beef and the rye bread or bagel. Then she'd make me the best tasting sandwich I'd ever had. Why? She wanted to make sure I wouldn't starve on the seven-minute drive home! Margaret Wolf, Caterer.

My name has often been a source of confusion, humor, and embarrassment. Early on, kids at school would exclaim, "Randi's a *boy's* name!" Kids would howl when they heard that my last name was Wolf. My father was not Jewish and therefore our surname was not Jewish. I had some bad experiences through the years. For example, someone would tell a "Jewish" joke not knowing I was Jewish. There was always that third party who would exclaim, "Randi's Jewish!" How embarrassing for a young teenager. I would often hear "You don't look Jewish." One day I went home crying about that. My mother said, "Next time, just tell them you forgot to put your third eye on." I don't think I understood that until years later, but I used it and it shut 'em up. Margaret Wolf, Diplomat.

My name became an icebreaker when I got older. "Randy" means horny in England. A consultant at work broke it to me for the first time when I was thirty-five years old. Since then, I hear it all the time in 007 movies and I've read it in numerous books. That explains why when I introduce myself with "Hi, I'm Randi," I get some interesting looks. I appreciate those looks now, so I always follow with, "That's a name, not a condition!" Did Margaret and Buck Wolf know that when they named me? It's hard for me to believe.

One pet name for me as I was growing up was Breckala. I, in turn, used that same pet name for my niece and nephew and a friend's kids. When I was forty and at a Passover Seder at a friend's house, I called one of the kids "Breckala." An elder heard me and asked if I knew the literal translation for "Breckala." I said no, and she told me it means "Little Crumb."

So throughout my childhood, was my mother purposely calling me a horny little crumb? I guess it could have been worse!

Chapter 4

The Neighborhood

Our segment of Hanover Avenue was a beautiful street lined with shady trees and small, well-maintained lawns and houses. There were Catholics, Jews, Baptists, Greeks, Native Americans, gay people, straight people, elderly, and young—and that was just within our city block. It was awesome. There could be no better neighborhood to grow up in. But no one labeled it "diverse." It just was what it was. I learned a lot about acceptance and coexistence from watching my mother's interactions with our neighbors. She enjoyed everyone. And all the kids on our block were my friends. To me, they were extended family.

I think most of the houses were built in the 1930s. They were disconnected row houses of varied architectural styles. I never realized how diverse our neighborhood was—not just the people, but also the buildings themselves—until I moved to the suburbs, with their cookie-cutter neighborhoods.

Margaret would sit outside on the stoop in front of the house and talk to the neighbors. One of her favorite neighbors was a Greek woman. Every Christmas, her family would have a party in celebration of her husband, Chris's, name day (December 25th being the Greek name day for Christ-derived names.) The pastries and food in general were unbelievable. So when the Greek Festival started in Richmond, I was already familiar with the food. They also had a pomegranate tree in their yard, so we knew all about that fruit when the juice "POM" came on the market.

There was a duplex to the east of our house. Two Jewish families lived there. One of the gentlemen simply could not park straight. Parallel parking was a requirement in the city. We laughed and he laughed at himself. Their son was Sherry's age. He was an outstanding tennis player. I remember comments surrounding the fact that he could never have played competitively at the Country Club of Virginia because—you guessed it—he was Jewish. One day in high school, several friends approached me and said, "You have got to see this hunk of a substitute teacher." So I went, stuck my head in the door, and the substitute and I exchanged a "Hi, Mike," "Hi, Randi." He was my tennis-playing neighbor.

Our neighbor to the west of our house was a lady from a prestigious "Old Richmond family" who represented the white Anglo-Saxon Protestant segment of the neighborhood. After her death, a very nice gentleman with mostly gentleman friends moved in. He was a horticulturist whose backyard was like something out of a magazine.

The neighborhood was full of kids, and we were automatically drawn to each other. One friend and I played in the playpen together. Others of us met and just began to hang out. Mothers were everyone's mothers; they all looked out for us. We would go from house to house eating Charles Chips when they were delivered by truck to our doorsteps. Those were the best potato chips. None of them were ever broken. They came in a large canister and were delivered every other week. They were a simple thing for the kids to look forward to. We would also snack on whatever each mother had to offer. One mom made the best homemade rolls; one made delicious desserts; and one always had ice cream and cookies. When my friends came to my house, they had chopped liver on a Ritz Cracker or a nice pastrami sandwich on rye. And they loved it.

In addition to the Charles Chips delivery, a local farmer would come by in his truck with fresh vegetables, and there was another farmer who would come by selling eggs. My mother loved buying from these men and explained the importance of doing business with our farmers.

At one time we counted thirty-five kids on our block. We were all shapes, sizes, and personalities. There was one person who lived around the corner whom we kids referred to as "girl boy." We didn't know anything about homosexuality, and my mother never made a point to tell me any details; I just saw her talking with her as she did with everybody else. One day Mama heard me say somebody was "queer." And in the mind of a ten-year-old (in those days), that meant goofy. Well, I learned a quick lesson. She told me I'd better watch out who I was calling queer. She said that one day I might say that to the wrong person and they might just knock me down. No explanation, just don't call anybody queer.

There were no black neighbors. A black lady came to our house about once every two weeks to iron. Now I don't quite understand why Mama, a "housewife," needed someone to come do our ironing. I suppose she disliked it (as much as I do today). Anyway, this lady sometimes looked after me. One day we walked to Cary Street. I remember walking down the street and passing a black gentleman. She did not speak to him. I asked why, and she said she didn't know him. I remember being surprised, as I thought that all black people knew each other.

Our mailman walked the route and he was black. On particularly hot days in the summer, Mama made sure I met him with a tall glass of iced tea. It was the nice thing to do. He was so appreciative. This was in the 1950s and early '60s, and Margaret Wolf was setting an example in very discreet ways.

During the civil rights movement of the '60s, Mama drove me downtown to see the lunch counter sit-ins at Woolworth's. At the time, I could remember there being "White" and "Colored" bathrooms in the department stores downtown. She pointed out how only white people were allowed to eat at the Miller and Rhoads Tea Room. She explained that the sit-ins were a way to fight against prejudice. She was teaching me history in the making—the best way to learn it. Margaret Wolf, Civil Rights Historian.

One day Mama read in the paper that a Ku Klux Klan meeting was scheduled that evening at some wooded area "in the country." She decided we would go. She wanted my sister and me to see what crazy people were like. I knew the KKK didn't like Jews, Catholics, or blacks. But hey, why not go and see if we lived to tell about it? We stood at a distance, more or less hidden in some woods. There were people running around in white sheets, as well as the expected cross on fire. I knew they were all cowards; otherwise, they would show their faces. All of a sudden, walking toward us through the woods, I saw the wife of one of Mama's brothers, and several of my cousins. They were Catholic. We laughed so hard! We were all there out of curiosity. One of my cousins proudly displayed her necklace with a cross, and we decided she should hide it. I'm sure if there had been a Nazi convention somewhere near Richmond, we would have attended that as well. Margaret Wolf, A Little Bit Crazy.

One of my friends was Catholic. We lived within walking distance of three Catholic schools: an elementary school, a girls' high school, and a boys' military high school. Nuns and priests lived there as well. We weren't intimidated by the nuns or priests; we knew some of them simply as neighbors. One day my friend and I were playing tennis at the girls' high school. A nun who was my friend's piano teacher came outside. She asked me if I played the piano and I said, "Yes, ma'am" like a polite southern girl. When she left, my friend was aghast: "Never say 'yes, ma'am' to a nun! You must say 'yes, Sister.'" Well, after she calmed down, I reminded her that I was her Jewish friend and didn't know the "Catholic protocol."

This same friend was very religious. She went to confession every Saturday. I mean, how much does a twelve-year-old have to confess? I often walked with her to the church, and before I went, I would open the front door and yell to my mother, "I'm going to confession!" She would say, "Okay," and just laugh and laugh. So I schlepped with my friend the three blocks to the church. I sat outside on the steps while she confessed. All the way home I would beg her to tell me what she confessed, but she never would. She was very devout. She did share this: "Forgive me Father, for I have sinned. It has been"—in her case—"one week since my last confession." That was the preface.

I guess Catholics weren't allowed to go to synagogues without special permission. When I was confirmed, her father asked for special permission from the priest to take her to my confirmation. My mother was quite impressed.

That same Catholic friend in later, adult years told me she had confessed adultery once when we were tweens. We had played spin the bottle with some boys in the basement and she thought this constituted adultery. I'm sure the priest got a chuckle out of that one.

In our house, the wall next to the stairs leading from the first floor to the basement became a graffiti wall for the neighborhood girls. We kids would write the date, our names, initials, jokes, and our latest thoughts on that wall. My mother refused to paint over the writing, and it was still intact when we sold the house. One of the girls from the neighborhood bought the house, and her scribbling was all over the wall. I wonder if she ever painted over it.

A few of us kids were young entrepreneurs. In the summer, no one could stop us. We wrote a neighborhood newspaper and sold it door to door. The neighbors always supported our endeavors. We wrote and presented plays, had restaurants, carnivals, performed takeoffs of television quiz shows, and on and on. We were very creative, and our mothers all encouraged us. Mama pulled out the sewing machine to make "waitress" outfits when we presented the neighbors with a restaurant venue one summer. We had a menu and we cooked on the grill. I was one of the waitresses. We charged admission for every event we had. Counting the money at the end of the day was the best part.

When it came to our performances, we often staged them in our backyard, so we were constantly running back and forth fetching supplies from the house. One play was "Murder at Midnight." Mama and Daddy both helped us with that performance. We thought it was the coolest thing when we received permission to bring a telephone outside to use as a prop for the play. Can you imagine unplugging a telephone and taking it outside? And after all the preparations and rehearsals, my father was at the premiere. He laughed for months later at the fact that I was killed in the first two minutes of the first scene. That was my short-lived acting career.

Once a week our gang would get together to play card games. We'd meet at a different house each week. One of the things that really tickled Mama was to look outside on the night of the game and see four or five eleven-year-old girls coming from all directions, each carrying a set of poker chips.

We kids would run up and down the street all day long. I suppose even in the early '60s we knew not to talk to strangers. When I was nine or ten, I noticed a car with two men in it parked in front of a neighbor's house. It was there for a couple of days. I finally mentioned it to my mother. She explained that we were going to have some visitors from Russia. They were cousins, and we were on their visitation itinerary for just a couple of hours. These men were making sure our family looked like law-abiding citizens. They were probably from the FBI. In my mind we were famous! I wonder if one of them was J. Edgar. In the end, I guess we were deemed no threat to national security. The cousins were very nice, and even spoke some English.

Chapter 5

Mama's Friends

Mama had many girlfriends. Like her, most were daughters of immigrants and thus first-generation U.S.-born Jewish citizens. She was good at keeping in touch with her friends and family and talked on the phone much more than I ever did as a teenager.

Mama loved to entertain. She would plan her menu and prepare the glassware. She had a collection of tulip wine glasses that she enjoyed using when her friends came over. As I recall, they didn't actually drink a lot of wine; they mostly drank champagne and screwdrivers. Many of the glasses were gifts from one of her girlfriends. My sister and I still laugh at the way her friend helped Mama collect these glasses: she would give me a glass for my birthday or Hanukah, graduation, or for any special occasion. She did the same for my sister. So Margaret's collection continued to grow as long as Sherry and I celebrated birthdays, Hanukah, graduations, etc.

Mama's entertaining was usually with family and thus casual. It could be a poker game with five or six people or a cookout with an uncle and aunt. She was in tune with her guests' likes and dislikes. Whenever we feasted on steamed blue crabs, Mama made sure she grilled hamburgers for those who didn't enjoy picking crabmeat from the shell.

My birthday parties were held at the house or the bowling alley. There were usually six or seven girls in attendance and one boy. My mother called him “the sheik,” and of course he and I had no clue what that meant. Mama planned lunches, games, and activities for all of my birthdays. She enjoyed it so much, I ended up having birthday parties until I was twelve, well past the age when most of my friends had ceased the practice.

When I was confirmed at age sixteen, she invited friends and neighbors and family. It was a major celebration with a great mixture of folks. She had delicatessen platters, rolls, potato salad, other foods, and of course a cake. When I graduated from high school, she had another party. And she would always have people over to celebrate holidays. Sherry and I were always included in the gatherings, and Mama would take advantage of her captive audience of guests to brag on us: Sherry got her driver’s license; Randi got straight As. Basically everyone would eat, drink, and smoke cigarettes, which wasn’t a problem, as Mama had an ashtray on every flat surface in the house.

Mama was always ready to help her friends. When he was about twelve, the son of Mama’s friend Dora told his mother he wanted a set of drums. He couldn’t have them because they lived in an apartment and it would have been too noisy for the neighbors. Mama and Daddy discussed it, and the next thing I knew, a set of drums was in our basement for him to come by and practice on periodically. Of course my daddy and I took advantage of the drums’ idle time and thoroughly enjoyed drumming away. Dora’s son continued to study drums through school. It paid off, because in the world of jazz, he’s now a famous avant-garde jazz drummer. His parents are deceased. I have tried to get in touch with him with no success. I know he would appreciate these memories of his “getting started.”

One of Mama's friends owned a grocery store. She would take me with her when she went to visit. Most of their conversations were about who had died, who was sick, and who was incapacitated. One thing this lady always complained about was her butcher. She said the butcher would stuff steaks around his belt, cover them with his jacket, and steal them from her. I heard that story at least ten times, and each time I had to prevent myself from laughing. I also remember this same friend coming to our house and cooking for us several times when Mama was in the hospital for a hemorrhoid operation. It was very nice of her to do that. Once Mama came home, the family had some chuckles over the operation as she sat comfortably on her "donut" cushion.

Mama frequently took me to visit her friends. She seemed to be the one who reached out the most. Her friendships were individual; I don't recall there being a group of ladies going out for ladies' nights. Most of the gatherings were in someone's home. Mama could always make her friends laugh. This was important, because many of them appeared depressed. There were several widows, and most of the ladies had grown up during very difficult times. Mama had a special place in her heart for one of the ladies who was single and had no kids and lived alone (little did I know then that for fifteen years between marriages, I would fit this same description). Many of Mama's friends had grown up on Church Hill; some were ladies she had worked with. One of her best friends was actually her second cousin, so they had family ties. All of her friends were different, and she maintained lasting relationships with all of them. She used to tell me that as I got older, it would be more and more important to maintain my relationships. I learned a lot from her example. Her friendships were genuine and stood the test of time.

Chapter 6

Who's Afraid of Margaret Wolf?

WHENEVER MARGARET WOLF COMMITTED HERSELF to a project or a job, she was dedicated to the end. She didn't consider failure to be an option. One of her strongest personality traits was that she was not at all shy and would present her grievances to anyone, anywhere. When she called, visited, or wrote, somebody always took notice.

Mama worked at home during my early years. She conducted radio surveys over the phone for a company called Hooper Radio Surveys. A friend worked for them and recommended my mother for the job. She was paid per survey, so she needed to keep people on the phone long enough to complete the questions. That was not a problem for her. She scheduled the surveys several times during the day. Whenever I was home and heard "This is a Hooper Radio Survey, were you listening to the radio when your phone rang just now?" I knew it was time to go upstairs. She was diligent about her work. Prior to beginning her calls, she would be very optimistic that people would take the survey. She'd sharpen at least twenty #2 pencils in preparation for filling out the lengthy form numerous times. I suppose she was successful, because she sharpened pencils every day!

When I was fourteen, Mama went to work outside the home at the DMV. I had never before needed to unlock the front door upon returning from school, so she taught me how to use the key. Coming home to an empty house took a little getting used to, but I got over it. She worked at the DMV for about seven years. One day she came home and said she had been offered a supervisory position. Daddy and I thought it was great. Not her! She said she told them she wasn't interested in any "title" if there wasn't any money to go with it! I do believe she got that job and some money eventually. One of her coworkers told me once that at work, people would say, "Who's afraid of Margaret Wolf?" a spoof on the play title *Who's Afraid of Virginia Woolf?* I thought it was funny, and it made me proud that she worked hard and stood her ground.

When I was young, Mama was published in the Richmond newspaper. At one point, for reasons I don't recall, her father was staying as a patient at MCV, a hospital in downtown Richmond. Mama would go to visit him. Since this was downtown, there were stoplights and pedestrian crossings with electronic "WALK" and "DON'T WALK" signs at the intersections. She would wait for the "WALK" sign before proceeding across the street. Mama got tired of being halfway across the street when the sign changed to "DON'T WALK." It changed too quickly. Well, she'd had it and decided it was time somebody knew how annoying it was. So she wrote to the *Richmond Times-Dispatch / News Leader* and suggested in her short letter to the editor that the sign should not say "WALK" but rather "RUN LIKE HELL." And it was published. Margaret Wolf, Advisor to the City of Richmond.

Mama did not take too long to make a decision or to retract one. My parents bought a new Ford in 1965, when I was thirteen. It was a standard with the gears on the column. That was strange to begin with. Mama could not drive it. It was funny and sad at the same time. I was in the back seat jerking left and right and trying not to laugh. With Mama in the driver's seat, a cigarette hanging from the corner of her mouth, and my father riding shotgun with his lips locked, I knew it was the beginning of the end of that car. Within a week it went back to the dealership with some interesting words, I'm sure. She came home with a nice new automatic and a smile. Thank goodness, because I learned to drive in that car.

Chapter 7

Music

Music was a staple in our household. My mother enjoyed all types of music and my father listened to opera sometimes. I assume their love of music resulted from the Hyman get-togethers of days gone by, when Grandpa played the mandolin. A new generation of music entered our household in the '50s, when my sister began to listen to rock and roll. And I enjoyed Motown, which was widespread in the '50s and '60s. Sherry had Elvis pictures posted on the living room bannister, and Mama loved it. It was new and exciting, so she didn't worry about how the house looked.

After an enlightening musical debut via the fourth-grade recorder, I decided I wanted to play the violin. Mama had a cousin who was the conductor of the Richmond Symphony and was reputed to be a musical genius. He offered to loan me a violin. We went to visit him in the Fan District to pick it up. He lived upstairs in a duplex and as we walked upstairs, I remember looking at hundreds of sheets of music stacked on the stairs. I knew I was going to become a famous violinist because I thought the talent must surely run in the family.

I heard my parents laughing as I practiced, but never to my face. My biggest claim to fame was being the president of the orchestra in the sixth grade and leading the orchestra during a PTA concert. In my mind, I was leading the symphony. My mother was so proud.

I'm sure she thought she was raising a virtuoso.

I took piano lessons between nine and twelve years of age. I liked it well enough and actually did pretty well. I had a piano recital each year, and Mama would let me invite a couple of friends to attend. Afterward, she'd take us to the Clover Room for ice cream.

Now, a formal piano recital with its practices and inherent anxiety is one thing, but I enjoyed the added pressure that comes with having a doting Jewish mother. When any of her girlfriends came to visit, she would ask me to play a song on the piano. I would play and then quickly retreat to my bedroom where I'd analyze the piece and how well I'd done. That was worse than a recital. I stopped taking lessons in junior high as I was simply too involved with school activities to make time to practice piano.

Another time I caught my mother chuckling in the next room: I was singing (a cappella) some of the more religious Christmas carols because I wanted to be in the Christmas chorus at school. I had to try out for it. I didn't make it, which I suppose was a "blessing" for a Jewish kid.

A radio was always on in our kitchen. Our stereo and its turntable were in the dining room and spun a lot of tunes, too. My mother listened to Janis Joplin, among others. I remember finding, in our dining room buffet, an album whose artist told off-color jokes. I, of course, had to listen to it. My mother was so embarrassed when I confronted her with it.

The Beatles made their British invasion when I was twelve. It was next to impossible to buy their first album. I wanted it badly, though it was a wish I didn't expect to come true. But Mama found a way to order it and it came in the mail. When she handed me that package, I had no idea what was inside. When I opened it, I was as thrilled as if the Beatles were right in my living room. Margaret Wolf, Very Cool Mom.

She always marveled at how I knew the words to every song on the radio. Had there been karaoke at the time, my girlfriends and I would have been there. By the time we went to junior high and high school, we "were" the Supremes and the Four Tops and the Temptations and so on. Motown was it! My first date was to a Temptations concert.

Well, the Beatles never made it to Richmond, Virginia. But the Dave Clarke 5 did when I was thirteen. They were the next best thing at that time. My mother took several neighborhood friends and me to the earlier of two shows offered one evening at a theater called The Mosque. It was fabulous.

Afterward, I was having a sleepover with my friends. Around nine P.M. my mother said, "Okay, girls. Let's go down to The Mosque and see the Dave Clarke 5 when they come out of the late show." Of course we were giggly and excited and ready to roll. We jumped in the car and laughed all the way.

When we got to The Mosque, lots of people were gathered on the Main Street side with the same idea as my mother. Her intuition kicked in and she said, "Not here, girls. Let's go around the back." We were the only fans back there. There were limos, so we thought we were in the right place. And sure enough, they came out that exit. There was a fence between us and the band members, but we saw them very close. I remember picking up a piece of rock to commemorate that moment at The Mosque. Cool mom. Smart mom. Margaret Wolf, Teacher of the Simple Things in Life.

Chapter 8

The Holidays

"The Holidays" took on a unique meaning in the Wolf residence. There were Jewish celebrations, Jewish high holy days, secular holidays, and Christian holidays. We celebrated most everything.

We always had a Passover Seder. We read the Haggadah and went through most of the traditional rituals. We always laughed at the part that read something like "drink the wine in a reclining position." Manischewitz wine was a Passover staple. I drank grape juice until high school and then I switched to wine. At one seder, Mama had to excuse herself and go up to her bedroom. She had a "spell." The truth is, she was tipsy from the wine. She was never much of a drinker.

The children's thing to do on Passover was to find the hidden matzo. Sherry hid the matzo in our house. Most of the time, it was just me looking, but I do recall a younger cousin looking one time. I believe I helped her find it and proclaimed her the winner. There was a monetary reward of fifty cents for the child who found it. So most years, I lucked out.

Passover falls near Easter most years. I always had an Easter basket full of candy and surprises. It was another secular celebration during which my mother didn't want us to feel left out.

My family's observance of Rosh Hashanah and Yom Kippur,

the two holiest Jewish days, changed over the years. When I was young, I remember getting dressed up to go to synagogue. Mama would pull down several boxes from her closet shelf. They contained beautiful hats. She would choose one to wear to Temple. We would go to the Beth Ahabah Temple for both observances. Rosh Hashanah is the Jewish New Year and it is a holy, somber event. Yom Kippur is the day of atonement for sins. You fast during Yom Kippur and after the fast there is a huge meal. Mama let me eat during the day because she said, "You don't have many sins to repent." After I was confirmed at age sixteen, Mama no longer paid her dues, and thus did not receive a ticket to come to the Synagogue on standing-room-only-days. So, we stopped going to Synagogue on holidays.

Halloween brought the usual question: "What am I going to dress up as?" My mother liked Erma Bombeck. She read an article in which Erma suggested that a kid could carry some magazines and go as a magazine salesman. She thought it was humorous, but we never used that idea.

We always came up with something. Halloween in our neighborhood was a lot of fun. One Halloween evening, my sister, my daddy, and I were sitting at the kitchen table. All of a sudden, the door to the basement burst open and out came an elaborately outfitted witch. She pranced around for a few minutes. It was Mama! She said she had been working on the costume in the basement for weeks. She went trick-or-treating around the neighborhood without revealing her identity. She was the talk of the neighborhood until they finally figured out who the witch was.

The next year, the neighbors were waiting for an encore. All I was thinking about was getting candy. I was probably eight or nine. We were walking, and she said she had left something on the stove, so we proceeded with another mother while Mama rushed home. Sure enough, she showed up with hose over her head, and I can't remember the rest of the costume. Margaret Wolf, the Halloween Surprise of the Neighborhood.

Our Christmas mornings were as exciting as they were for any Christian child. Even before I was born, Santa Claus came down the chimney in our house. He was a part of my mother's religious evolution, as she balanced her Orthodox upbringing with her desire to give her daughters every joy life had to offer.

I have hilarious memories of my mother trying not to admit that we celebrated Christmas. She sort of rolled with the punches and Daddy had no issues with it. We could have a Christmas tree, but it had to be placed in a corner of the dining room so that it was not visible from the street. Through the years, we had a silver tree with revolving lights, we had artificial trees, and we had cut trees. They were always placed in the dining room corner.

We could not put any Christmas lights in the windows, because Mama didn't want any outward displays of celebrating Christmas. One evening, Mama went to the store and my father and I put two candelabras in the window as a joke. Candelabras! They didn't even resemble the typical Christmas candles. She came up those front steps three at a time. You would have thought we had set the house on fire! She wasn't even in the door before we heard, "Take those candles out of the windows right now!" She didn't appreciate the joke.

My uncle Herman's wife, Fage, was very Orthodox and more reserved than the rest of the family members. She gave us Hanukah gifts, and I remember receiving from her beautiful books about Jewish holidays and Jewish stories. She was very nice and carried on conversations with me. One day I was sitting in the living room and Mama was on the phone. As soon as she hung up, she yelled, "Move the Christmas tree to the basement! Aunt Fage is on her way over!" Sure enough, we moved that tree to the basement and when our aunt left, we brought it back up. Standard Christmas operating procedure.

After Christmas one year, she asked Daddy to drag the tree to the trash cans at the end of the yard and to do it at night. She didn't want the next-door neighbors, who were Jewish, to see the tree. Daddy did just that. The next morning we were eating breakfast and we looked out the window at the backyard. It was covered with tinsel! Those neighbors really didn't care, but Mama continued to hide the fact that we celebrated Christmas even in the secular sense. Christmas must have been one of the most stressful times of the year for her. But she wanted to make us happy, and at that time I suppose we thought it was important to celebrate most everything.

In 1961 I was ten and in the fifth grade. I was an angel in the school Christmas pageant. Mama made the most adorable costume for me. I remember she even used the sewing machine. And naturally, being the angel that I was, I comfortably took on the role without a hitch.

Of course, we also celebrated Hanukah. According to tradition, as the youngest child, I would light the candles, and we would receive a gift for each of the eight days. So basically, we had it made in the gifts department. On the first night of Hanukah when I was about nine, I dutifully put the candles in the menorah and was looking around for a yarmulke (skull cap) to cover my head. It's very important to cover your head. There were always some yarmulkes in the drawer in the dining room buffet, but not that night. What had happened to the yarmulkes? Who stole the yarmulkes? There were none to be found. Mama hesitated for a moment, looked at me, and the next thing I knew, she put a pot holder on my head and said, "Light the candles."

To this day, when I light Hanukah candles, I feel a special warmth in covering my head with something other than a yarmulke.

Chapter 9

The Weekends

Among other practices in the Orthodox Jewish religion, one does not work or drive on the Sabbath. The Sabbath runs from Friday sundown to Saturday sundown. Mama never cooked on Saturday. I never questioned it, but retrospectively, this may have been her way of obeying the Sabbath. Saturday dinner was fend-for-yourself. But Sunday dinners were special.

Most Sundays, Mama would cook one of her specialties, and Uncle Herman would come at precisely two o'clock. His favorite meal was chicken soup with matzo balls. I think it was everyone's favorite. After the meal, we would go to the living room to watch football when it was in season. Mama loved football, and we of course loved the Redskins. I think she understood football pretty well, but she couldn't comprehend why they would send a running back straight into the middle of the defense. She liked a passing offense. Imagine a Hail Mary pass to a well-covered receiver. He catches the pass under extremely close coverage. She would jump up and exclaim, "It's as if that ball had *eyes*! Go, man!"

For the longest time, I was under the impression there were only two football teams: the Washington Redskins and the Greenbay Packers. Somehow, they always seemed to be on our TV.

While on the topic of sports, I'll mention that I have no recollection of watching any baseball on TV unless it was the World Series. Then, it was standing room only in our living room. Why?

Because every chair and table was covered with those betting pool sheets that Mama had invested in.

If ever there was a time Mama's cigarette was hanging out the corner of her mouth, it was when she cheered watching sporting events.

Mama considered professional basketball boring. If you asked her why, she would say there were too many slam dunks. "It's our turn and then it's their turn. It's our turn and then it's their turn. They're all too good." If she could only see athletes today!

Chapter 10

Pastimes

My mother loved playing cards and games, gambling, and entering contests. She especially enjoyed strategy games, which challenged her mind. Since she'd grown up with seven siblings, competition was a way of life for my mother. Now that she was an adult living in *her* home with *her* family, the competitive nature she developed as a child could be applied to activities she enjoyed.

Poker nights were frequent at our house, with aunts, uncles, and friends joining in. I observed them for a few years and was invited to play around age ten. Sometime prior to that, I learned how to play Go Fish, rummy, canasta, and solitaire.

Poker night at the Wolf residence went like this: Mama would prepare the nosh for the evening. She would set out beer, soft drinks, and iced tea, peanuts or mints, and sometimes sandwiches. If it was a hot day, she would make sure the air conditioner was on full throttle. She would put on some comfortable slacks because (finally) pantsuits were in style. Sometimes we used pennies and sometimes we used poker chips. One night someone won all the pennies and they had to resort to betting with matchsticks. After that, Mama always made sure she had the poker chips available, just in case. Before we could begin a poker game with the penny antes, we had to close the front curtains because Mama stressed, "it is illegal to have money on the table." Our dining room was visible from the front porch but not from the street, so her concern was unfounded. Not to mention, I doubt there was ever more than five dollars on the table, and all in pennies!

I don't know why, but the games were so loud! It was like a yelling match. Everyone was having fun, though. Mama always had words of wisdom to share. She just loved the game and didn't hide her enthusiasm. Whenever the bet was going around the table and everyone was "checking," Mama would always yell out, "I didn't come in here checking!" In a poker game, if one declares "check" when it's her turn to bet, it means she wants to see what everybody else is going to do before she declares her bet. Mama thought it was the sissy way to proceed, so she declared her bet as soon as the bet came to her. I suppose I have my mother to thank for my gambling interest. Yes, she taught me Go Fish and Old Maid and the kids played canasta, but I suppose gambling is in my blood.

Every week she entered a newspaper contest called Cashwords. It was a crossword puzzle with an interesting twist relative to solving the puzzle. Because of this twist, there were limited winners. It was very strange, to tell you the truth. It was in the Saturday paper and there were cash prizes. After poring over the puzzle, Mama had to cut the puzzle out of the paper and glue it to a postcard and mail it to the paper. Every Thursday night we would hear "Get off the phone! The Cashwords man is trying to call me." He (whoever "he" was) actually made a phone call to the winner. Unfortunately, he never called us.

A Richmond radio station always had interesting contests. For one contest, when I was eight years old, the DJs provided clues every so often throughout the day. You were trying to find a vial hidden somewhere in Richmond. If you found the vial, the prize was an oil well. Yes, an oil well!

Mama listened to the radio to gather the clues. After several days' clues, she piled a few of my sister's friends and me into the car and said she knew where it was. We were on our way to Dogwood Dell, an outdoor amphitheater. We searched for a while throughout Dogwood Dell, and yes, we found the vial. It was at the bottom of the amphitheater as I recall. We were all screaming and jumping up and down. Mama of course said, "Let's take this home before we lose it!"

News reporters came to our house; she was on the news, the radio, in the paper, all the local media. It was a very exciting time. I remember thinking, "We're going to be rich and I can get all the Barbie clothes I want."

After all of the publicity and the excitement, the radio station reported that they had dug and the well was dry. There was no prize. My mother was absolutely humiliated, but she never looked into getting a lawyer or suing the station. All she requested was that we no longer listen to that radio station in the house. Margaret Wolf, Classy Lady.

Years later I ran into the radio announcer who worked for that radio station and who had been to our house to interview my mother during the oil well debacle. I asked him if he remembered the oil well contest. He said, "No, we only gave cash prizes." Who knows? But I did notice he had a big diamond ring on his finger! Randi Wolf, Gutsy Lady.

When I was around nine or ten, we would go to Maryland, meet Mama's sister Rose, and take a ferry ride to a place called Marshall Hall. I had never been on a large boat before, so it was fun just getting there. The boat was huge and people were packed in. Gambling was allowed only in certain areas of Maryland. We had to take the ferry some distance into the Potomac River, past Virginia boundaries and into Marshall Hall. The sole purpose of the trip was to provide a venue for my parents to play slot machines. When we arrived, we immediately went into a building with no amenities other than the machines. It was not a child-friendly place, so to amuse me, Daddy let me pull the lever. After a short while, we were asked to stop because the minimum age to play was sixteen. The machines dispensed coins and it was okay for me to gather those. The coins clattered loudly and the day was exciting. I looked forward to turning sixteen so I could play. They closed down just before that birthday. That was my first introduction to real gambling, and to this day I love a slot machine. Mama always wanted to go to Las Vegas, but she never made it.

She always had a jigsaw puzzle laid out on the dining room table. Everyone knew to try to insert a piece or two whenever they walked through the dining room. Once it was completed, it went back in the box and she moved on to another one. She played board games, too. I never beat her in Scrabble. She was unbelievable, and I always checked her words.

We bowled a lot. It was duckpin bowling, in which you used smaller balls and threw three times. Duckpin bowling was a regional game found mostly in Virginia and Maryland. You could get a score of ten in a frame. My mother could deliver those balls perfectly. You couldn't even hear them hit the floor. For my ninth and tenth birthdays, she arranged parties for me at the bowling alley. The alley had a room for parties, and they would "cater" with hamburgers and so on. I suppose Mama was one of the first mothers to host "destination birthday parties." I usually invited six or seven neighborhood friends, so we all honed our bowling skills early on.

We didn't take many vacations, but we once went to the Rappahannock River and stayed for a week in a chalet. We were with an aunt, uncle, and cousins. There must have been holes in the chalet, because we all were eaten up with mosquito bites. Upon returning home, Mama said, "We would have been better off grilling hamburgers in the backyard. At least we would have planned to use *Off!*"

We enjoyed fishing and often went to a pier near Buckroe Beach. Daddy taught me how to put a worm on a hook when I was young. He also bought me my own rod and reel when I was eight or nine.

When Sherry was sixteen, my parents took six of her friends with us to Virginia Beach. We'd rented an apartment there for the week. Once again, I was one of the gang. Mama thoroughly enjoyed cooking for everyone and feeding all the boys from TeeJay who hung out at the apartment. The girls played a joke on one of their male classmates. They told him to come by the apartment. They were going to fix him up with a cute girl named Randi. He appreciated the joke. That week was not really a vacation for my parents, but they enjoyed being with all the young people.

Mama liked the theater. The Virginia Museum of Fine Arts housed a theater known as Theatre Virginia. There were a variety of presentations and most of the troupes were travelling. I remember getting dressed up and going to some performances, but I do not remember the titles. We also went to The Mosque to see some very well-known shows. I specifically remember *The King and I* and *Fiddler on the Roof*. Mama also took me to the Richmond Symphony, as her cousin was the director for several years. And she and I went to see Dionne Warwick at the Richmond Coliseum together.

She loved for me to give her manicures while watching television. She made the best TV snacks in the world. She could take whatever was in the fridge and create a masterpiece of a presentation on the coffee table.

One thing she did for herself was a weekly or biweekly hair appointment. She said that having her hair done, and I quote: "makes me feel like a new person."

Her favorite television show was *All in the Family*. She was one of its more dedicated viewers. News with Walter Cronkite was a daily routine, and other favorites included Ed Sullivan and Johnny Carson. When we got our first color TV, she was more excited than I was when *The Wizard of Oz* came on once again. This time we were going to see it in color. We thought the brand new TV was broken because the movie was in black and white, but then Dorothy arrived at Oz!

Collecting S & H Green Stamps was a pastime we all enjoyed. When you bought groceries from participating merchants, at the end of your transaction you received a certain number of green stamps based on how much you'd spent. I think you received one stamp for every ten cents you spent. You pasted the stamps in a collection book for safekeeping. Your goal was to fill enough books to redeem them for products at the redemption center. The more stamps you collected, the more valuable the products you could choose. There was a catalog of products you could review at home. It felt like you were getting something for free when you redeemed your stamps. Mama would collect a few "books" and we'd go to the redemption center several times a year. She usually had something in mind that she wanted to get, but sometimes she'd turn over the stamps to my sister and me. You could choose toys or even a small appliance with enough stamps. There were mostly household items, and there were sports items. I recall buying several things to take to college.

One day after hearing us talk about it so much, Mama wanted us to take her to this "McDonald's place" so she could see what it was all about. She wasn't impressed, because it was a walk-up and you had to eat in your car. But she was pretty hip, so she didn't want to remain uninformed about this latest establishment.

Chapter 11

Mama's Cooking

Mama was a great cook. She particularly enjoyed making Jewish dishes and southern comfort food. My favorite dish was matzo balls, which are dumplings that must, and I repeat *must*, be served in a bowl of delicious chicken soup. Mama found them tedious to make, but not too terribly so, because she made them quite often. Today I can buy matzo balls off the shelf as supplied by Manischewitz, a Jewish foods distributor.

My second favorite dish was kreplach, which is a ravioli-type dish that is also best served in chicken soup. It was painstaking for Mama to make. If she were to have written a cookbook, the first entry for kreplach would have read, "Preparation time—one day!"

First she would create the dough and knead it and roll it out until it was the perfect consistency and thickness. She would brush beaten egg across the dough in order to ensure that it would stay together. Then she made the stuffing. She would boil chicken with celery and onion. While that was cooking, she would prepare to use a manual grinder. She'd place the grinder on the side of the table and attach it to the table with a lever. Then she'd feed chicken and onion into the grinder and crank it by hand. Due to the grinder's limited capacity, this took at least an hour.

Finally, after the grinding was done, she would return to the dough. She cut the dough into squares about two inches by two inches and meticulously placed a spoonful of the chicken on each square. She folded each one into a triangle and carefully pressed the sides to seal the chicken in. She always made at least thirty, so as to make it worth her time. She then boiled them until the dough was done. The finishing touch, of course, was serving them in her delicious chicken soup.

She made kreplach soup several times in the winter and sporadically throughout the year. Even at a young age, I would eat two or three bowls in a sitting. I have never tried to make kreplach, but my sister has indicated an interest, so together we may one day recreate Mama's kreplach. Fortunately, both Sherry and I have mastered chicken soup.

The following are a few of her other specialties:

Fried salt herring – Delicious, and you could feel your arteries drying up as you ate them. This was a Sunday breakfast item.

Brisket – A stereotypical Jewish cut of beef. Mama was a "one-pot" cook.

Hard herring – Raw herring that she cut up, added pepper and onions to, and served as an appetizer. Sherry and I call it Jewish Sushi.

Gefilte fish – An acquired taste made of pike fish. She would buy it and doctor it up and bake it.

Chicken soup – This needs no explanation. Often referred to and recommended by doctors as Jewish Penicillin, it is guaranteed to cure you of whatever ails you. There was a specific way to eat Mama's chicken soup. She prepared the noodles, broth, and chicken separately. So you would put noodles in your bowl and pour chicken soup on top of them. The chicken would be served on the side.

Matzo balls – Made from matzo meal, it is a Jewish dumpling. It goes in chicken soup. It, too, was difficult to make from scratch.

Chopped herring – Famous for this dish, Margaret purchased special herring, which required soaking overnight. She used a hand grinder to mix the herring, hardboiled eggs, onions, bread crumbs, and other ingredients. You ate chopped herring on crackers as an appetizer. Never on bread.

Chopped liver – Another Margaret specialty, this was cooked liver chopped finely and mixed with some type of fat and hardboiled eggs. Chopped liver on a Ritz Cracker was an absolute delicacy. Today you might hear it referred to as "liver pâté."

Chuck roast – A very common Sunday dish; my sister and I called it "chunk chuck."

Cabbage and potatoes – Another one-pot specialty.

Borscht – A beet soup you ate cold with potatoes and sour cream.

Fried chicken – Another Sunday staple, Mama's was the best I ever had.

Sauerkraut and beef – An acquired taste that was developed through the years.

Matzo-meal pancakes – They were sweet and you didn't need syrup.

Potato latkes – A Hanukah staple, these are potatoes prepared in pancake form.

Chinese tea – It was awful.

Bagels, cream cheese, and lox – Even I could make that!

Though Mama could have been the Margaret Deen of Jewish dishes, she also made more "normal" foods like pork chops, steak, hamburgers, and awesome spaghetti.

She was not a baker. She made one cake—a boxed lemon cake made in a Bundt pan that she would top with her sweet "drizzle," which was made of sugar, milk, and vanilla. Other than that, she loved Dot's Bakery on Cary Street.

As I said before, she was an ambassador for anything instant: instant coffee, instant potatoes (they were awful), canned goods, etc. She never lived to see a microwave, but if she had, she would have been first in line to buy one.

Unfortunately, she suggested I not hang out in the kitchen whenever she cooked, so I learned few special recipes from her. I suppose she thought I'd marry a rich man and have a cook. My sister, on the other hand, did learn some of the recipes, and she has coached me on a couple of the dishes.

I do remember Mama showing me how to make biscuits from scratch. I was probably seven. She pulled up a chair close to the kitchen counter and stood me on it. She showed me how to measure the flour, add the milk, and knead, knead, knead the dough. Next I learned how to flour the rolling pin and roll out the dough. She gave me a juice glass to use as the cutter, and so I proceeded to cut out the biscuits. I placed each one on a baking pan. When all the holes were made, I mashed the dough back together and rolled it out again until it had all been cut. Mama put them in the oven.

I remember thinking how easy it was. Daddy took the taste test when they were done, and of course he just raved about them. Right then, I knew that one day soon I would make those biscuits by myself and surprise my parents. So a week or so later, I decided to make biscuits on my own.

I got up early on a Sunday morning before my parents were up and went down to the kitchen. I couldn't reach the counter, so I pulled up a chair to stand on and began to create those biscuits. I was kneading and kneading and I didn't notice my mother and father watching me in the doorway. Apparently I had an itch on my bottom and reached down to scratch it with my floury hand. My father busted up laughing and announced that I had redefined the term "biscuits from scratch!"

Chapter 12

Religious School

Orthodoxy prevailed in my mother's heart, perhaps even more so because of the Holocaust. Daddy accepted Judaism, sort of went with the flow, and looked to Mama to raise Sherry in the religion.

When Sherry was five, it was time to begin her religious education. So my parents sent her to an Orthodox synagogue and Sunday school. It was a dreary, dark building, and Sherry found it frightening. The way the male congregants engaged in their prayers was a bit eerie to a child, and everything in the service was spoken in Hebrew. Most Orthodox kids had learned some Hebrew at home by Sherry's age, but she had not. She had no idea what was going on in the service. She hated it and cried each week.

Mama paid attention to Sherry's grief. She decided she needed to make a change for her little girl. She was going to join a different synagogue. There were three synagogues in Richmond: Beth Israel (the Orthodox temple), Beth El (a conservative temple), and Beth Ahabah (a reform temple). My family lived around the corner from Beth El, but Mama decided to skip over the conservative option and joined Beth Ahabah downtown.

Once she was convinced to try Sunday school again, Sherry enjoyed it much more. She was drawing pictures and singing songs. It was a much more comfortable environment for her. The inconvenience was a sacrifice for Mama, but her daughter's happiness prevailed.

When it came time for me to receive my formal Jewish education, my parents sent me to Beth Ahabah as well. I attended it from the second grade through my sophomore year of high school. I think my mother waited until I was in second grade to send me because she was a little gun-shy after my sister's initial experience.

I never liked religious school. It was stressful. I had to study, for goodness' sake! Even my mother laughed at how I'd walk out to catch my carpool ride to temple with more books under my arm than I carried to school.

I attended religious school on Sundays until my confirmation year at age sixteen; that year, I attended on Saturdays, as part of our education involved going to services. I finally enjoyed some of the discussions during my confirmation year. The rabbis led some of these classes, and I suppose I preferred listening to a PhD in theology over a volunteer teacher.

Keeping in mind that this was the reform synagogue, for some reason it attracted all the wealthy Jewish families in Richmond. So I never felt like I fit in. I resisted every week, but I always went. I remember drawing names for Hanukah gifts in the third grade. I did not receive a gift. I guess the kid who drew me didn't come that week. I was devastated. I believe the policy of "bring a gift, take a gift" started the next year. We would sing "We wish you a Happy Hanukah . . ." to the tune of "We Wish You a Merry Christmas" and kids would bring Hanukah gifts wrapped in Christmas paper turned inside out. That's when I realized we weren't the only Jewish family who celebrated Christmas at home. As I got older, the kids talked more about Christmas than Hanukah.

My mother was room mother one year and had to bring foods related to various holidays. I was always nervous, because I was sure she would say something to embarrass me. And after all, I didn't really like being there in the first place. She never embarrassed me at all.

Of all the religious-school teachers I had, one stands out in my mind. He was my fourth-grade religion teacher, and he explained to us in simple terms the basics of Judaism. I also remember he sent gifts to everyone in our class when we were confirmed.

When I was about fourteen, a boy from my religious-school class called and asked me out. He was from a very well-known family. I didn't like him and declined. This was something I never discussed with my mother, trust me!

When I was confirmed, everyone in my confirmation class gave a speech before the congregation. The topics were provided to us. Aside from an oral book report, this was my first presentation to a large group. Knowing the significance of this assignment, I prepared extensively for it. I received kudos for it, and that was the end of religious school. Amen.

The best thing my mother taught me about Judaism is that you don't need to sit in a synagogue every Friday night or Saturday morning to respect your religion. I learned that Judaism resides in the heart and the family. Margaret Wolf, Theologian.

CHAPTER 13

Life's Education and Formal Education

TIME WAS MARCHING ON. I graduated from elementary school and spent much of the summer preparing for seventh grade in junior high school. I was maturing. I had begun to develop an interest in some of the neighborhood boys. Instead of playing basketball with them, I found myself standing on the sidelines watching. These boys were the ones I had avoided earlier for fear of getting cooties. Mama once told me it was okay to be smarter than the boys, but don't challenge them in sports.

I was petite, self-conscious, and horrified when anticipating the locker room in the seventh grade. I needed to get a bra; that was a given. I didn't say I *needed* a bra, just needed to *get* one. So, Mama and I went shopping for one. It was not painful at all. I made it through the seventh grade without a hitch and continued to get good grades. This was the year to make new friends who had come from other elementary schools. It was not unusual for me to bring friends home after school. Everyone lived in the general neighborhood. After a few meetings with one girl, Mama said, "She's a little too fast." I didn't know what "too fast" meant at the time, but later I had to admit that her insight had been right on. Indirectly, she taught me to pick my friends wisely, as we are judged on the people with whom we choose to associate.

I got braces in the seventh grade. As if I wasn't self-conscious enough, now I had a mouthful of wire. They were actually not bad, and many of my classmates had them. My mother was very particular about the doctors and dentists I went to, and if she liked them, she *kept* them. When I was fourteen, I wanted to get my ears pierced. Mama took me to the best plastic surgeon in town! When I was a sophomore in high school, I found out that a friend of mine was the son of my doctor. The problem? I was fifteen and still seeing his dad, the pediatrician. I told Mama I needed to move on. When I was nineteen, my wonderful dentist told me I needed to graduate to the adult dentist across the hall.

Then in the eighth grade, one of my classmates invited the entire class to his parents' river cottage for the day. "Bring your swimsuits," he said. My poor mother. I was a wreck. I didn't think the swimsuit I had was appropriate because it wasn't a two-piece. No problem. My mother found a pattern and made me the cutest two-piece bathing suit I could have wished for. Margaret Wolf, Seamstress.

I became a cheerleader in the eighth grade. While some of the cheerleaders didn't understand football, I had my mother and father to thank for my grasp of the sport. I was able to coach the squad on some of the basics of the game, such as why and when we were to yell, "First and ten do it again!" It was natural for me to want to cheer. After all, my mother was a Redskins cheerleader every Sunday.

Eighth grade was the year when the girls took home economics. First, we learned how to sew. We made aprons. That summer, I must have made my mother ten aprons, all of which she graciously accepted. In home economics we also learned about nutrition. I recall going home and berating my mother because I thought we were not eating nutritionally sound meals. At least not according to my textbook! At that point, she could have whacked my behind and responded with some choice words. Instead, she gave me a "watch it, young lady" look and then chose to review how some of our recent meals were, in fact, nutritionally sound. She even referred to my textbook.

When I was younger, if I acted up, my mother would get angry with me and yell, "Get upstairs and clean your room!" Sometimes I even received a slap on the behind. This lasted well into my teen years. But as I grew up, when it came to uncomfortable topics, she used a less direct approach. Over the years, I learned to read her signals and gestures out of necessity.

When I began menstruating, I went to her, and she went to her closet and pulled down a large box. She handed it to me and told me it included everything I needed. She was right, but I remember feeling sad. Obviously, she had planned for this day by purchasing the material. She'd probably had it for a year or more. I had also planned for this day, but with hopes of having an intimate conversation with Mama. She relied on school and pajama party conversations to ready me!

I had close to a unibrow in that awkward tween period. She presented me with tweezers one day without saying a word. She did lighten the moment by also giving me my first blush-on.

One day we were at the Beacon Bookstore on Cary Street. I was just browsing, as was she. I found a book whose title implied it had to do with the facts of life. I knew them already, but not from any discussion with my mother. So I decided to play dumb and show her the book very inquisitively. She grabbed that book and paid for it in two minutes flat. I took the book home, and it was about hens, roosters, and fertilized eggs!

Both my parents smoked heavily. It was amazing the quantity

of cigarettes consumed in our household. I would sneak a couple of cigarettes now and then and smoke in my room. I thought I was hiding it pretty well. But one night when I was sixteen years old, we were having a family dinner with an aunt and uncle. We had finished eating and everyone was lighting up. Very nonchalantly, my mother said, "Randi, please don't hide your ashtray under the bed." I was so embarrassed, I ran upstairs and stayed there the rest of the night. It was easier for her to say it in front of the group than it was for her to address me directly.

She wasn't the only one to employ that tactic; Daddy used it too, though a little more gently. My father gave me sips of beer at an early age, so drinking alcohol was really no big deal. I had little need to experiment with it much in high school, but I did like the taste. In our early teens, my friends and I discovered a clandestine way to obtain beer. The grocery store sold beer in small refrigerator-sized returnable kegs. Mama bought them. My father spent a lot of time in the basement working at his workbench, so the keg was placed in the basement refrigerator for easy access. Well, the neighborhood gang and I would enter the basement from the outside and tap that thing every now and then. I guess we were tapping it a lot harder than we thought.

One evening at the dinner table, Daddy told Mama that she needed to take the keg back to Safeway because they'd sold her one that was half empty. Another indirect confrontation; I kept quiet, and we didn't tap that keg anymore.

When it came time to start high school, I was to attend Thomas Jefferson. Thomas Jefferson High School was known as the top high school in the state and one of the best in the country. The teachers' credentials were outstanding, and the students were exceptional as well. "TeeJay," although public, was of the caliber of a private school. To attend TeeJay, some students traveled across town from other school districts. I received an excellent education and had a few particularly good teachers who taught me to appreciate writing.

Clothes were very important to me in high school. Whenever Mama and I went shopping, we argued. Mama took me to department stores and boutiques. We could never decide on anything. I often came home empty-handed. Yet every now and then, she would go out and buy several dresses or skirts and bring them home to me, and I would always like what she picked out. I could never explain it. Margaret Wolf, Fashion Coordinator.

I continued cheerleading and thoroughly enjoyed high school. Mama and Daddy were supportive in everything I did. Doting mother that she was, Mama would ask me to do a cheer in the living room when she had visitors. Unlike the piano requests when I was younger, I would politely refuse these requests.

Mama was proud of me and let me know it, even if indirectly. One time she came to a football game. After the game, she told me I looked very cute out there cheering, but she had a suggestion: "Keep the pom-poms out of your face so everyone can see you." Margaret Wolf, Jewish Mother.

At the end of the year, the school had an awards dinner for all of the athletes and the cheering squad. Parents were invited and Mama went with me. It was in the school cafeteria and very nicely catered. Coaches spoke and presented awards. Two of the coaches knew my mother from when Sherry went to school there, and they always greeted Mama when they saw her. When she walked into the room, we were met with several calls of "Hi, Mrs. Wolf!" She was well liked. I felt like I was her guest instead of the other way around.

High school sororities were prevalent in Richmond-area schools, though they weren't officially recognized by the schools. The schools supported boys' clubs such as Hi-Y and Key Club, as these were service organizations; but while the sororities did some community service, they mainly concentrated on "sisterhood" and social gatherings. They held meetings at various members' homes and attended beach week each year, and they were very cliquish. There was an all-Jewish sorority whose members were from various Richmond schools. In addition, there were three TeeJay sororities. I identified them by what I now understand to be stereotypes, but what the heck. They were: the "fast" girls, the WASPs, and the "nice" girls. I was invited to join all four of the sororities. In the past, the "WASPs" club had been known to purposely exclude Jewish girls. I panicked upon receipt of the invitation. They must not have known I was Jewish, I thought. I asked a friend whose sister was in the sorority about this. She said they had "changed the rules" that year and hoped I would join. I was flattered, but mostly insulted at the same time. I did not accept. I had always known I wanted to join the "nice" girls' club, which I did. My sister had been a member.

Because the sororities were unrecognized by the school, pledging was interesting! One day I came to school with my unwashed hair in pigtails, sporting lots of makeup, a long skirt that was not in style, a shirt that didn't match, and whatever else I was required to wear. Mama helped me get dressed and said I looked great as I walked out the door. Well, my homeroom teacher almost sent me home. She said: "Are you pledging a sorority, Randi?" "Yes, ma'am." I probably would have been suspended had I said "No, ma'am, why do you ask?" She said, "Well you'd better go clean yourself up." I did the best I could and made it through the rest of my classes.

I enjoyed those years in the sorority. It was a diverse group of girls, with members from a variety of religions. I never told Mama I had been invited to join the Jewish sorority and declined. Again, that was something not to be discussed with my mother. Considering how she had mellowed, she may not have cared. But why bother her with it? She liked the girls in the sorority I joined.

Sweet sixteen and ready to drive! Some of our most heated arguments involved Mama taking me out to practice driving. We went to an affluent area named Windsor Farms, where everyone learned how to drive. The streets could have been renamed to "Slow Down Road" or "Brakes! Avenue." She and I could not work together on this. We lasted five minutes before I pulled over. I got out of the driver side, she got out of the passenger side, and without discussion we switched and drove home with her behind the wheel.

Now, my father was a different story. He took me to Windsor Farms, all right. He led me right through that neighborhood and out onto Cary Street, a busy street. Then he led me onto a side street that was about as wide as the car. But I found our way home safely, delivering the car in one piece.

So I began driving. My parents were generous about letting me use the car, especially considering that we had only one. One day I was prepared for quite a confrontation when I came home and told my parents that the car needed two new tires. How did I know? Well, my oldest friend and I were cruising in her car when we came upon a police checkpoint. She cautiously drove through it. She had her license and the car registration, so there was no problem. As driving novices, we found any driving-related escapade amusing. We enjoyed driving up and down two inclines at a Holiday Inn; we enjoyed driving down Riverside Drive, which was curvy and ran alongside the James River; we would ride through the University of Richmond and slowly drive past the fraternity houses; and we would drive through the nickel toll booth and pay for the vehicle behind us if it was a car of boys. So this checkpoint was something new, and I just had to drive through it for the experience of it! We went home so I could get our car, and I drove to and through the checkpoint. In my case, though, the policeman didn't want just a license and registration. He told me we needed two new tires. But I lucked out. My daddy said that was good to know, and he would handle it. He did ask where the checkpoint was and why I felt compelled to drive through it. When I explained that it was "something different," he just smiled.

What were my parents' wishes for me? Of course they wanted me to obtain a good education; that was a given. But they also wanted me to enjoy my time off. So in the summers, while everyone else worked, I slept late, did a little babysitting, hung out with high school and neighborhood friends, spent time at Virginia Beach, watched soap operas, and practiced cheerleading for the next year's tryouts. I realize now that my parents, and my mother in particular, wanted me to have the fun and relaxation that was denied them in their youth.

Chapter 14

College Days

In the fall of 1969, I was a senior in high school. The Vietnam War was as its peak. The war never seemed real to me. My life was not directly affected by it, and as a result, I stayed rather oblivious. It seemed like a blurry backdrop to my daily, stress-free life. Most of my friends and I were preparing for college, and the boys were not thinking about the armed forces. We were definitely in a bubble.

It was time to decide where I wanted to go to college. I knew I had to go to a state college and that was fine with me. After all, Virginia has some of the finest. I applied to a couple of all-female colleges at the time, Mary Washington and Longwood, as well as William and Mary and Virginia Tech. The University of Richmond/Westhampton was not an option, as I knew I wanted to leave Richmond. I was accepted to all except for my first choice—William and Mary. They put me on the waiting list. And you know what? They still haven't called!

I chose Virginia Tech because it was coed. My mother, father, and I went to the bank to apply for a college loan. We all signed, and it was approved on the spot. It would cover the tuition and books, and my parents would provide spending money. That day was a banner day, because it was my initiation into the world of adult responsibilities. I knew I had to make good grades and pay back the loan once I graduated. I also received a teaching scholarship that helped with expenses. The deal was I had to teach for four years in Virginia, and that's exactly what I did.

Never having been to Virginia Tech, my sister, my mother, and I visited it for an orientation. My mother and sister shared a dorm room. Mama was very uncomfortable in the bunk bed and could not sleep. Sherry reported that she sat up all night in a chair. My mother never uttered a complaint about it. She was a trooper the next day in spite of having had little rest. We all fell in love with the campus, and that's where I invested the next four years.

My graduation from high school was a major celebration. Mama invited her friends over, and I went out for a celebration with my friends. She gave gifts to all of the neighborhood friends who were graduating from public and parochial schools. Most of us were off to college, and I knew she was going to miss all of us. I cried through most of the graduation ceremony.

In 1970, the summer after my graduation, a friend invited me to go to Miami Beach with her family to visit her grandmother. It was my first flight; my parents paid for my ticket. I don't know how they were able to pay for this, considering college was just around the corner. They sacrificed once again. I was very nervous about flying. My daddy assured me that the plane ride would be so smooth, I could drink a glass of water without spilling it. I went, and thoroughly enjoyed the flight. A week on millionaire's row, a cabana at the Fountain Bleu, maid service, and all the luxuries were quite pleasing as well. It was thought provoking at age eighteen to see how the very rich live.

As I prepared for college and bought clothes, it was exhilarating to buy slacks, "cords," and jeans. In high school, we could not wear slacks or even culottes. Thinking about wearing jeans to classes was new and exciting. Mama, on the other hand, wondered, "Will girls ever look like girls again?"

Margaret decided my clothes should be labeled so I wouldn't lose them at the "laundry mat" on campus. She ordered labels that simply read "Randi Wolf" and sewed one in each article of clothing! I didn't think much of it. As far as I knew, everybody did it.

It was August 1970 . . . Virginia Tech, here I come. When I arrived at Tech, my roommate was very funny and easy to get to know. She'd gone to a prestigious girls' school in Tappahannock, Virginia, where she boarded. Thus, she laughed and laughed about the clothing labels and other "never been away from home" quirks of mine.

Several months into the school year, Virginia Tech's first-ever successful panty raid was executed on our freshman dorm. How exciting it was. I was down the hall, but my roommate was in our room, sitting on the top bunk. She later reported that when a young man from the neighboring dorm worked his way into our room, opened my drawer, and grabbed a handful of intimate apparel, she yelled, "Drop it!" It startled him, and he did indeed drop everything and run out. That would just be a normal panty raid story if it weren't for the fact that my dear roommate saved me the embarrassment of having my intimate clothing items strewn around in a boys' dorm . . . with my name sewn in each one!

As if getting used to being away from home and finding my way around the huge Tech campus weren't stressful enough, I was flunking Biology 101. The professor taught as if we were medical students. It was one of those lecture classes with three hundred students. I did indeed fail the class, and since the grades were posted, it was clear that more than 50% of the students flunked along with me. Most of them were freshmen. Well, after my hysterical report to Mama over the phone, I still can't believe what she did. She called T. Marshall Hahn, president of Virginia Tech. Obviously I didn't hear the conversation, but I can imagine. And I heard the professor was later put on probation for flunking too many students. Margaret Wolf, Advisor to the President.

I was an elementary education major. I called home every Sunday. My parents would pick up two different extensions so all three of us could speak at the same time. When I reviewed my first quarter's classes and got to badminton, my normally subdued father said, "What? How much am I paying for you to play badminton? We play badminton in the backyard!" I explained about my three required physical education classes, and I had to describe how vital it is to place the birdie within six inches of the top of the net to really make a good play. By that time, we all three were laughing and he calmed down. In subsequent quarters I took tennis and archery, and these settled better with Daddy.

I was the only girl on my hall who received "care packages" every few months. My mother regularly sent me a box full of snack items and other necessities. I always shared with the girls. I used the linen rental service and had mentioned that the sheets were not very comfortable. My sister sent me a set of *Peanuts* bedsheets to use. They were special coming from her, and of course we all read *Peanuts* in the newspaper. My neighborhood friends and I exchanged mail regularly. I would get one or two letters a week. I quickly discovered exactly how wonderful all of this was, because few girls in my dormitory enjoyed such connections to home.

I had a checkbook, but the statements went home. I never felt deprived, and I learned how to handle money pretty well. I also had a charge card at Leggett's, the local department store. I never used it without telling my mother first, and sometimes she would suggest I go buy this or that. I look back on my roommates, several of whom were from wealthy families. They had to "prepare" to call home and ask for money. My parents didn't want me to worry about money (remember their backgrounds), and as a result, I think they trusted me to be conscientious.

During summer and other breaks from school, my college boyfriend, a couple of his high school friends, and I would rent a U-Haul trailer and pile into his very old sedan for a road trip. We would head to Richmond to drop me off on their way to Chesapeake. When we arrived at my house, Mama would have a buffet fit for kings set out on the dining room table. She'd be all ready for "the boys." She knew they must be starving. Through the years, "the boys" and my mother became good friends. Her buffet was the talk of Virginia Tech.

My aforementioned college boyfriend was Catholic. He was studying to be an architect. He would bring his latest drawings to show my parents, and they were very impressed. Catholic? No problem. I'm sure the reason my parents liked him was because an architect would make a good living. It didn't matter, because we eventually broke up. His final words to me were "I hope your mother doesn't hate me."

When I was twenty, Sherry and her husband, Gene, had a baby girl, Alison. This was by far the most excitement our family had ever experienced. My mother had assumed she would only have a grand-dog, as Sherry and Gene had been married five years before having Alison. Mama and Daddy took care of the baby several times a week. They would put Alison in a carrier and place her on the kitchen table and just coo at her for hours. When they moved to the living room, Mama would carefully place the carrier on the floor. If it was next to a table, she would slide back anything on the table. That way, gravity would be less likely to pick up an ashtray or a lamp and drop it on the baby.

I loved coming home from college to see the newest member of the family. At times I was a little jealous because—well—I wasn't getting all the attention. Daddy detected this in me and I wasn't proud of it. Let's face it: I was twenty years old! He took me upstairs and opened the bottom drawer in his bureau. He pulled out pictures I had drawn specifically for him when I was a kid, along with other masterpieces from my childhood. I was amazed. He simply said, "I've kept these all these years. I wanted you to see them."

For my senior year in 1973-74, Virginia Tech decided elementary education majors would student-teach the entire year. The fact was, they were insightful. The need for teachers is cyclical, and unfortunately we were in a period when that cycle was down. They were trying to make us more marketable.

Three roommates and I decided to live in Roanoke since we were all student-teaching there. We were so responsible! Only one of us had a car. Well, after one quarter of living in Roanoke and basically forsaking our senior year on campus, we became less responsible. We moved back to Blacksburg. We were lucky to find an apartment. Now we had one car traveling round trip between Blacksburg and Roanoke daily. And I might mention that the oil embargo and gas lines were the top newsmakers at the time. My dear parents told me to go buy a car. They gave me a budget, and I did it. They made the payments until I began teaching, and again I realize how they struggled for me. After I bought the car, I called them with the details. It was a two-door 1974 V8 Pontiac Ventura, green with black and white plaid seats. It was hot! The next time I talked to Mama and Daddy, they said they had driven to a local

Pontiac dealership to see the car. They thought it was gorgeous.

That fast car got away from me one trip home, and I received a speeding ticket. This time Mama was very direct: "I will be humiliated when this citation crosses my desk." She worked at the DMV!

I had just turned twenty-one and was home from college for spring break. Mama and I met a friend of hers for dinner. She wanted me to have a cocktail with them since I was twenty-one, but I had left my ID at home. We lived about ten minutes away, and she insisted I go back home to get my ID. I did, and she was thrilled that we were able to celebrate my "legal status" with a *l'chaim* toast that evening. The simple things in life.

I graduated from Virginia Tech in June of 1974. Now, my mother couldn't settle for a casual graduation celebration with the immediate family. She invited my Aunt Glen, Uncle Virgil, and three of my closest neighborhood friends to go to Blacksburg for the graduation. She and Daddy also paid for hotel rooms for everyone. They spared no expense.

At this stage in their lives, Mama and Daddy had experienced two events that were simply dreams coming true: the birth of a granddaughter and my college graduation.

I began teaching in August of 1974. I was living at home. I've often heard that the first year of teaching is extremely hard, and mine was no exception. I would stay up into the wee hours preparing lesson plans, checking papers, and just trying to stay ahead. Mama would stay up with me, just to keep me company. She would put out some nosh for us and sit in the living room. I worked in the dining room where I could spread out my papers. She was a great assistant, as she helped grade papers for me.

One night as we sat up together, I talked about my struggles in the classroom. The plumbing at the school kept going out, leaving us without water; I had to buy supplies out of pocket because the school didn't have them; I had kids in my sixth-grade class who could not read and write, but I also had a child who ultimately went to the National Spelling Bee, and everyone in between. Welcome to teaching. My student-teaching experience had been utopian. Virginia Tech had not prepared me for the realities of the job.

Mama listened and asked me if that school system was right for me or if I should look elsewhere for the next year. I shrugged and continued working. I couldn't think about anything but the next day at school. She was tired, but then, it was late. I asked about her back, because she had mentioned that it was bothering her at work. The doctor had suggested she avoid working directly beneath the air conditioning vent. I thought that was a weak solution. She used a heating pad sometimes while sitting on the sofa. She said it was a little better that day. She rarely complained. She finally went to bed and I continued on, grading papers late into the night. Little did we know that cancer was already growing inside her.

Chapter 15

Words of Wisdom

Mama offered tidbits of wisdom and advice that I'd like to share. Some are practical even today; some are outmoded; and some are strange. I will attempt to explain those that are not obvious:

- *When someone dies, send a "Thinking of You" card instead of a "Sympathy" card.* She thought the words "in sympathy" were cold. "Thinking of you" is more personal.
- *Read the obituaries every day so you'll know when you need to visit or send a card.*
- *Look at yourself whenever there is a conflict.* She could always tell when something was wrong between a neighborhood friend and me. The first thing she would ask me was, "Ok, what did *you* do?" This, combined with Jewish guilt, means that to this day, I have a built-in mirror.
- *Study hard, get a good education, get a good job, and then marry a rich man.*
- *Bumble Bee tuna is the only safe tuna.* There was a tuna scare of some sort years ago and Bumble Bee tuna was not affected.

- *Don't drink milk with fish.* I have no idea.
- *Don't eat barbecue in the summer.* In hot weather, pork must be handled carefully so it does not go bad.
- *Chinese food is chicken chow mein.* That's the only "Chinese" she ate.
- *"Don't worry if you girls don't have a date for the weekend. The boys don't have any money."*
- *When buying your mother a gift, please do not give her anything "for the house."*
- *It's ok to compete with boys as far as grades are concerned, but try not to beat them in sports.*
- *If you're hungry, eat a bagel. It will hold you over.*

Chapter 16

Saying Goodbye

In the fall of 1974, Mama went back and forth to doctors trying to determine the source of her worsening back pain. She began to lose a lot of weight. The doctor scheduled her to go to the hospital to run some tests. On Monday, December 9, she left for the hospital with the understanding that she would be there for a couple of days. She could barely walk. I stood on the sidewalk as my brother-in-law and uncle helped her down the steps and into the car. My mind had gone blank. I think I was still in denial about how bad off Mama looked. She checked in to the hospital and we got her settled in her room.

On Tuesday the doctors performed an exploratory exam. Basically, they opened her up to see what they could find. My sister and I were there when she returned to the room, and she slept most of that day. We didn't know when we would receive the results of the exam, but it would likely be that evening. Sherry and I never discussed the possibility of Mama dying. Although she was thinking it, she wouldn't burden me with those thoughts.

At some point, Sherry had to go home to check on her daughter, and I stayed with Mama, reading a magazine and watching to make sure she was okay. One of her neighborhood friends was an

R.N. at that hospital. She stopped by. She asked where Sherry was and I told her she had gone out for a while. She could have been fired for what she did next, and she did our family a tremendous favor without even knowing it. She whispered to me, "The results showed inoperable pancreatic cancer." She said she had looked at the chart. She said the doctor would call Daddy later that evening.

I almost fainted. I felt nauseous. My knees were weak. I said, "Cancer? Mama was never sick a day in her life."

Mama was asleep, so I ran to the car to go home to call Sherry and Gene. I could hardly see, I was crying so hard. I couldn't bear telling Daddy on my own, and the doctor was going to call him any minute. I knew I needed Sherry and Gene to be there with us when he got the call. Daddy was in the kitchen, so I went upstairs to use the phone. Sherry and Gene came over immediately. We knew Daddy would be devastated, and I think all of us worried that he might suffer a heart attack upon hearing the news. When the phone rang, Daddy answered, and the three of us huddled around him. The doctor told him she had pancreatic cancer and she had three to six months to live. My father suddenly looked frail and helpless. He almost fell to the floor. He exclaimed, "Oh my God! Mama! No! No!" Gene helped steady him and walked him to a chair. We were all crying hysterically. We finally put Daddy in his bed and left him to cry himself to sleep.

Mama was scheduled to be in the hospital another couple of days, and then she would come home for those three to six months. We visited her and never mentioned the diagnosis. Someone called her siblings and several visited in the next day or so. When her youngest brother, from whom she'd been estranged, walked into her hospital room, Mama looked up and said, "I must be dying." I believe she knew before the doctors did that she had cancer. In the hospital she never asked what was going on. She knew; there's no doubt she knew. I would help her with her daily rituals by brushing her hair, plucking stray hairs from her chin, and putting lipstick on her. She was emaciated and slept most of the time. It was a time to think about Daddy and how he and I were going to take care of her over the upcoming months. Somehow we needed to prepare ourselves for her death. I knew Daddy wouldn't handle it well. And somehow we needed to make the most out of the three to six months Mama had left.

Then, on the morning of Friday, December 13, 1974, just four days after Mama checked in to the hospital, the phone rang early. I went to the hall and picked it up. It was her doctor. He said my mother had passed away. I was numb, but I knew I needed to call in the family support once again. I had to worry about Daddy before myself. I called Sherry and Gene. Daddy was in his bed, and we asked Gene to visit with him and break the news. I could hear him scream once again. He loved his wife dearly and was dependent on her. Now his world had been upturned. He had always been the sick one; Mama had never been sick for more than a day. They always thought he would go first.

Bliley's Funeral Home made the arrangements for her burial. We chose to have a closed casket and offer the usual visitation hours for people to pay their respects. The idea of standing in a funeral home greeting people when he was in such terrible pain was too much for Daddy. He couldn't do it. Sherry and I performed the duty. The next day we had a service at Bliley's prior to the funeral procession. She was buried in a Hebrew cemetery in Richmond's East End.

When we were en route to the cemetery, I stared out the car window and wondered how those people on the street could possibly be laughing and frolicking when my mother had died. Surely they should be mourning with me. The rabbi who had confirmed me presided over the burial. Afterward, people gathered at my sister's house. She and I had shared one chuckle the night before. She was rushing to clean her oven because friends and relatives would bring food to reheat the next day. Sherry said, "Mama would turn over if she thought I had a dirty oven for everyone to see."

That day went by in a blur. I don't think Daddy was at my sister's house.

Once everyone left Sherry's, I drove home. I dreaded it. I dreaded going into that house with Mama's things all around. I dreaded Daddy's depressed state. I dreaded only having a couple of days to get myself straight before going back to school. I dreaded, I dreaded, I dreaded. Daddy and I were alone in the house. It was winter, and the house felt empty and cold. Mama's absence was different now. When Mama was in the hospital, we expected her to return. I cried myself to sleep with a pillow over my head so Daddy wouldn't hear. He struggled to just get out of bed each day. He did not try to act like he was doing okay for my sake. He grieved and grieved.

It was a horrible time for all of us. Sherry, Gene, and my boyfriend were always there for me, but naturally, those weeks after Mama's death were all about Daddy. He was our number-one priority. Gene was so wonderful to him. He spent numerous hours with him, and Daddy loved him like a son. My father's mourning didn't abate. He began to spend a lot more time in his bedroom. Friends and neighbors brought food constantly for weeks on end. But Daddy was simply a lost soul. Sherry and Gene bought him a dog, which was a mistake. He never connected with it; he kept the dog in the basement and threw food down the steps. Gene finally rescued the dog from its misery.

I tried to attend to everything related to Daddy's health. I had observed how Mama cared for him. I made sure he took his medication properly and I tried to cook decent meals for him. We were both absolute wrecks. I was still teaching and had a major crying spell one day in the teacher's lounge. Sherry and Gene did as much as they could. They would bring Alison over to visit her grandpa, and he enjoyed those hours with her. I had friends who checked in with me, and I continued to see my boyfriend on a regular basis. He was to be my future husband. Daddy drank more than usual and I couldn't blame him. I wished I had an outlet to ease my pain.

On the morning of January 12, 1975, Daddy decided to make fried salt herring. He invited Gene to come over for breakfast. His breakfast hour was much earlier than mine and Gene came over around six A.M. At this point, he would have come over at four A.M. if it could have made Daddy happy. Gene was his strongest supporter. I was sleeping upstairs and was awakened by Gene yelling, "Randi, call an ambulance! Call an ambulance!"

I made the call and ran downstairs. Daddy was on the kitchen floor and Gene was trying to resuscitate him.

The ambulance came quickly and took Daddy to the same hospital where Mama had died. We went there, met my sister in the waiting room, and I exclaimed, "What the <expletive> else can happen?!"

The emergency room doctor on duty was our second cousin. He came out to tell us Daddy didn't make it. He asked if we wanted to do an autopsy. Sherry and I simultaneously said, "No." Heart attack would be the cause of death. But we both knew Daddy had actually died of a broken heart. He and Mama had died just thirty days apart, both just fifty-nine.

There we were at Bliley's again. We even had the same Bliley brother working with us. Arrangements were made for a closed casket and visitation, the service and the burial. As nothing is ever easy or straightforward with our family, there was one "problem." The managers of the cemetery did not want to bury Daddy next to my mother. It was a Hebrew cemetery, and he was not welcome because he never formally converted. Technically, I understood. But I found myself wondering, "How can Jewish people be so prejudiced and small-minded after what happened in Europe during WWII?" I was disgusted. My mother's brother Herman talked to the manager of the cemetery, and my father's burial was approved. I'm sure my uncle paid him off.

A young rabbi conducted the burial and I was very fond of him. Although I was numb and unfeeling that day, the rabbi took me under his wing before and after the burial. He soon moved to California. I was sorry to lose him, because for once I had met a rabbi who was truly approachable.

On the day Daddy died, I contemplated going back to the house by myself. I was heartbroken, and all I could think about was how unbearable that would be. But Gene was one step ahead of me. He would not allow me to go back to the house alone. That same day, he moved my bed and some furniture into a spare room in their home. That night as I lay awake in a new bedroom, I realized I was a twenty-two-year-old orphan. And much like an orphan, I was spending the night in a different house from the one I had grown up in.

I lived with Sherry and Gene for three years, including a move to the suburbs. The impetus behind their move was the school system. Unfortunately, the Richmond school system had deteriorated over the years. Subsequent to moving out of Sherry's home,

I lived in two apartments with roommates and then got married in 1978. The marriage lasted a short two years, during which time we bought two houses. I moved back into an apartment when we separated. So after spending twenty-two years in one house, following my parents' deaths, I moved seven times in seven years. Since Mama had never taught me anything about moving, I was proud to realize I had developed a new skill on my own—the ability to keep my furniture and piano intact through many moves.

After Daddy's death, I questioned my religion for a long while. I didn't really start feeling okay with it again until I reunited with a Jewish school friend in 1980. By that time, my divorce was in the works and I was experiencing a lot of feeling sorry for Randi: "I lost Mama; then I lost Daddy; now I'm getting a divorce; I don't have any kids; and I don't even have a solid career." I knew that particular friend would be able to relate. We knew each other's parents and she had known my mother very well. Her own mother had died when she was fourteen. She lived in Boston and I decided to find her. I called her aunt, who told me she was moving back to Richmond. She had married a non-Jewish man, so we had a lot of catching up to do. We got together one evening at her father's home, where I met her husband and her baby daughter. We clicked immediately and I liked her husband. From that day forward, we saw each other regularly. I credit her with helping me rediscover and appreciate our "Jewishness," if there is such a word. We cried together and laughed a lot. Yes, there is a thing called Jewish humor, and one must be Jewish to fully understand it. She helped me regain an appreciation for it.

For a long time after her death, I thought Mama's doctor had failed her by not taking her backache seriously early on. As a result, I developed a distrust of doctors and an increased vigilance toward any warning signs in my own body. When I was twenty-three, I found a lump on my breast and felt it, massaged it, prodded it, and did everything I possibly could to make it go away. A friend from college finally dragged me to the phone to make an appointment. I went to a surgeon. He told me I had "lumpy boobs," at which time I fell in love with his bedside manner. Still, he wanted me to have an outpatient procedure to remove a cyst. I did, and I was fine.

Even routine check-ups make me anxious. During a gynecological visit in my early twenties, my blood pressure was up, perhaps because I was so nervous. I told the doctor they should check your blood pressure upon leaving, not upon arriving! To this day, I worry until I've received my pap-smear results, and mammograms themselves are nothing compared to the agony of waiting for the results. Over time, I've learned that I inherited high blood pressure and high cholesterol from Daddy. They're both under control. But I can't stop thinking about that backache. If the doctor had taken it more seriously, could they have saved Mama? Probably not. Even today, pancreatic cancer is almost always a death sentence.

When I left teaching in 1978, I went into real estate. The classes I took prepared me well for the state exam. I passed and proceeded to work in a branch office where Gene was the broker in charge. I enjoyed it, but all good things must come to an end. Interest rates on loans rose drastically under the Carter administration, and selling houses was no longer a feasible option for me.

I decided to go back to school. I had some inheritance money that sustained me while I worked for Kelly Services as a temporary secretary and attended Virginia Commonwealth University's evening business school. I studied information systems. It was 1980, and that was the field to be in. To this day I don't know why in the world I thought I'd like programming. It was tedious and very frustrating. But I was committed, so I was going to see it through. Not to mention I needed a real job.

At age twenty-nine, I was hired as a programmer trainee by a local company. Eventually, I moved into computer systems training, and later, training management. I remained with the company for thirty years until I was laid off at age sixty. I experienced some humiliation and ego deflation over that, but now I am enjoying my retirement. It came two years earlier than expected, but at least every day is Saturday!

In the 1980s, Gene established a very successful home building business. Richmond's West End was the area of choice for his homes. After the seventh move, I decided it was time to stop renting, and Gene built me the cutest rancher in an area of Henrico County named Glen Allen. I was thirty-five and it was *mine*! For the first time, I was a truly independent woman. The house had a living room, an eat-in kitchen with beautiful cabinets, three bedrooms, two full baths, a fireplace, a deck, and an attached outdoor storage area. Gene's finish carpenter was the father of a former student of mine. That student was always in trouble. He helped his dad with some of the work on my house, and I half suspected there would be some type of booby trap built into the house somewhere, compliments of that young man.

My friends and family partied frequently at that house. This was where I started to enjoy entertaining. The first party was a surprise for Gene's fortieth birthday. I entertained mostly with beer in red plastic cups, not tulip glasses à la Mama. I lived in that house until I married Spencer Lauterbach, and now I rent it out.

After my divorce, I remained single until I was forty-nine. The childbearing years flew past me, and single life had its ups and down. I love to say I picked up Spencer in a restaurant. We were both waiting for other people for lunch; we exchanged business cards, and he actually called. Spencer and I were married on September 1, 2001, after dating for three years. He had been widowed at a young age and he didn't have children. We are reminded of those childless voids quite often. Whereas in earlier years I felt deprived because I didn't have children, today the absence of grandchildren is almost more hurtful. I am forever grateful for my niece and nephew, whom I was able to spoil through the years. I thoroughly enjoyed being a soccer and basketball aunt.

Sherry's life took an entirely different direction. Of course Alison joined the family in 1972. My nephew, Scott, was born on July 17, 1976. Sherry worked in the medical arena for many years. She did medical transcription, which required a keen knowledge of medical terminology and very fast typing skills. Doctors recorded their patient information, and she would transcribe it. She was paid according to how many transcriptions she did, and her fingers didn't just dance across the keyboard; they boogied. It was very lucrative.

Eventually, Sherry went into real estate and was quite successful once those interest rates came back down again. Gene continued to build in the West End. Both Alison and Scott were outstanding students. Their high school afforded them the same type of environment that Sherry and I experienced at Thomas Jefferson; it was cool to be smart and it was cool to be involved in school activities and sports. They went on to college—Alison to North Carolina State and Scott to Virginia Tech.

Today Spencer and I live in a fifty-five-plus neighborhood in Glen Allen, Virginia, outside of Richmond. We try to stay involved in community activities. Spencer deejays for parties and weddings and has provided music many times for community events. I have discovered an interest in the stage and am involved in a small thespian group whose mission is to provide entertainment for the community, while having fun doing it (I'm still loving that audience). A graduate of J. Sargeant Reynolds' School of Clownology, I sometimes perform as Breck the Hobo. I also enjoyed seven years as a house volunteer and a member of the Board of Directors for Richmond's Ronald McDonald House. Spencer has done volunteer work with Henrico County Schools and Henrico County Police. Life keeps us busy and we are very happy.

I'm sixty-one now, two years older than my mother was when she died. It's strange to realize that with any luck, I will continue to grow older, while my mother will remain younger than me, forever fifty-nine. On Sherry's sixtieth birthday, we were jubilant because she had broken the "fifty-nine curse." When I turned sixty, I, too, felt a sense of relief.

Throughout the past thirty-nine years, I have shared my experience with others who have lost loved ones by writing a short note in "Thinking of You" cards:

The sorrow you feel today soon will be replaced by laughter and fond memories.

There are still tears, but chuckles and smiles prevail. I miss her on Sundays. I miss her when I make chicken soup. I miss her always.

Margaret Wolf was a kind, intelligent, funny, and strong lady. By writing this book, I have learned more and more about her and her legacy to me. She taught me many things, but three lessons in particular have guided me throughout my adult life. Number one is to have a sense of humor and the ability to laugh at myself. Number two is to stand up for what I think is right. And number three is to not be intimidated by other people, no matter who they are.

I think my parents would be proud of who I am today. I know they would love my husband, Spencer.

About fifteen years ago, I ran into an old neighborhood friend at the grocery store, and she said something that will stay with me always. She told me I reminded her of my mother, and that my mother continues to live through me.

Thank you.

"Don is a true Renaissance man. This comes through clearly in *Winners and Losers.* Don masterfully succeeds in describing the mental and emotional mindset of successful entrepreneurs and leaves the reader with an all-new perspective."

—George Stalk, senior partner (retired)
of The Boston Consulting Group

"Why not confront the unvarnished truth and accelerate your success by learning from those who've actually 'done it'? But only if you really want to. *Winners and Losers* will provide you with the unvarnished truth."

—Mark Kramer, JD, board chairman of First
Hyperion, LLC and president emeritus, North
American Plastics, and Lt. Col. USMCR (retired)

"*Winners and Losers: Entrepreneurial Lessons from 30,000 CEOs on How to Come Out on Top* says it all in the book title! It is a masterpiece that will ignite your thinking!"

—Dr. Joe Pace, peak performance psychologist

WINNERS AND LOSERS

WINNERS AND LOSERS

Entrepreneurial Lessons from 30,000 CEOs on How to Come Out on Top

DON SCHMINCKE

Some names and identifying details have been changed to protect the privacy of individuals.

Published by Schmincke Learning Institute, Baltimore, Maryland
www.sagaleadership.com

Edited and designed by Girl Friday Productions
www.girlfridayproductions.com

Cover design: Megan Katsanevakis
Project management: Reshma Kooner
Production editorial: Laura Dailey

Image credits: cover © iStock/DNY59, iStock/Mironov Konstantin, iStock/4x6

ISBN (paperback): 978-0-9964102-3-6
ISBN (ebook): 978-0-9964102-4-3

To my kids, Rowan and Nolan,
for tolerating the entrepreneurial mistakes
of a father trying to change worlds.

CONTENTS

PREFACE

Before we start, I know this isn't your first book on entrepreneurship. You're expecting me to inspire you with the usual tips, motivational quotes, and success stories.

Well, that ain't gonna happen.

What I will do is expose rare, even controversial insights I've discovered by venturing into uncommon worlds. But you'll have to follow me into unfamiliar realms—anthropology, evolutionary psychology, genetic warfare, death-zone altitudes, neurology, and human instinct. Bring a shovel, because we'll be digging up the graves of our entrepreneurial ancestors. Better yet, grab a scalpel and let's perform autopsies on recently dead companies to find out why they didn't make it.

I know. Not your typical intro to a business book.

But hang on. I never meant to be doing this. I first tackled the sciences doing orbital satellite research at the Johns Hopkins Applied Physics Laboratory in the late seventies. Then I began studying planetary physics, computer science, and electrical engineering at MIT. To pay my tuition, I worked on nuclear missile guidance systems at Draper Labs.

Yeah, I'm a geek.

But something happened when I automated the Harvard/MIT biomedical engineering lab to do human experimentation . . . on myself.

There was an accident.

No. Not that kind of accident. That's for the sci-fi movies. I used my body to experiment on impedance shifts when

electrodes are applied to skin. Ever notice that when you get an electrocardiogram (ECG) at the doctor's office, they stick those electrodes on you? That's because of me. Well, not really me. I just happened to be the guy automating the lab and plugging into these weird machines to record my body functions. A lot of brilliant people took it from there. I did, however, co-publish my first paper on this in a medical journal, so I guess it was all kind of cool.

As I hung out in surrounding labs, I got accidentally exposed to a lot of experiments on human biology, including a room full of brains next door. So I thought, "What if I extended my studies to investigate humans?" And I did.

Humans became my favorite species! I even have a few friends who are human.

My fascination grew into the study of how humans group for work, play, replication, civilization, and war. I left MIT and began graduate work at Johns Hopkins University in the eighties. Eventually I ended up on the faculty, and then things got interesting.

Pulling Back the Curtain

While researching human organizational performance at Hopkins, I ran into a lot of executives in the MBA program. Many seemed cynical about management theory and the best-selling leadership books.

I asked why.

"We're tired of all these management consultants, phony experts, and self-proclaimed thought-leaders selling quick-fix, off-the-shelf solutions that never work."

"Bestselling, trending management theories sound good until you implement."

"Our company hired another management consultant, but my people are so cynical because of the high failure rates."

I did further research on this. Did you know there are over five million scholarly papers published on management theory failures?

This all got my attention, but what was I supposed to do?

An interesting experiment occurred to me. What if we forgot everything we knew and viewed business management like a rare activity on a newly discovered planet?

Look, I'm not a genius, but having the privilege of being around a lot of brilliant people helped. They guided me on how to study this planet as if I never knew management existed until I landed here. I dug deeper into discovering ancient and modern methods for leading humans.

Then things changed dramatically.

In this rare experiment, we unearthed surprising, counterintuitive leadership methods. But I kept running into a problem. Applying ancient methods and new bioleadership approaches in today's organizations often contradicts bestselling management theories. I wasn't very popular.

Johns Hopkins was very supportive of my research, though, and students loved the reported breakthroughs back in their office. Eventually I left to start my own executive education company—and risked funding my own research.

I had no idea what I was doing.

Not knowing how this was all going to work out, I created a couple CEO groups in the early nineties as a testing laboratory. They were very patient with me. Some were even crazy enough to let me experiment with implementing my discoveries so I could figure out what works and what doesn't. By using success metrics on sales growth and organizational performance, I kept only the methods that drove results beyond what CEOs had experienced before.

Then things got crazier.

I started doing expeditions to remote—and sometimes high-conflict—regions to study humans, expand my research, and continue connecting with brilliant scientists in different fields.

Often, people ask how I went from being a planetary physicist to an explorer and a rogue management researcher. No clue. If someone told me I'd spend the next twenty-five years training over thirty thousand CEOs in workshops and keynote speeches, I would've ordered what they were drinking. Today I travel 250,000 miles annually to keynote speak, work with company teams, and train seven hundred CEOs in over sixty cities. So, when you see a geek at the hotel bar with a laptop and scientific papers, I'm that guy.

Results

The laboratory experiment grew. My team and I began facilitating strategy retreats, leadership workshops, coaching, branding, organizational restructuring, and cultural transformation. This direct exposure to companies in over a hundred industries allowed us to track the results of our research. We expected to see a 10 or 20 percent increase in sales, profits, and organizational performance over twelve to twenty-four months.

But that didn't happen.

Instead, companies saw improvements of 200 to 300 percent, and in some cases 1,000 percent. Many became leaders in their industries. One year we had two clients in the Ernst & Young awards.

How long do these effects last? Our clients typically stay with us for ten-plus years. Strangers often approach me at

airports, like one afternoon as I was rushing through Chicago O'Hare after doing a sold-out three-day speech tour.

"Hey, Don! I want to thank you! I heard you three years ago and used everything in your speech," he said.

I had no idea who this guy was.

"Well, thanks for the feedback. Always great to hear we made a difference," I said and started walking away.

"No, you don't understand." He stopped me. "I just sold my company last month for $10 million because of a lot of the ideas you gave me. I'm going to keep following everything you're teaching. Especially when I start my next company."

I stood there stunned. Quiet. Smiled. Then thanked him again, shook his hand, and proceeded to my gate.

But when did my focus shift to entrepreneurs?

The Shift to Entrepreneurs

Several years ago, a CEO asked why I hadn't applied these methods to transforming entrepreneurship. She said a lot of people are trying to start their own company, or grow the one they already had, or be intrapreneurs to drive change inside their organizations. I told her there were already thousands of books with millions of copies sold to entrepreneurs. But she said, "Yeah, millions of books sold, but why aren't there a million more entrepreneurs?"

She had a point. Failure-rate data. Hmmm. I'd been here before.

That initial thought turned into the book you hold in your hand now.

I never set out to expose entrepreneur myths. That happened when I realized all the books talk about taking risks, planning, learning from mistakes, systems, models, finances,

failing fast, HR, being positive, leadership styles, etcetera, but none risked asking whether entrepreneurs really fail because:

- These expert tips may not work for everyone.
- We are only addressing the symptoms, not the deeper problems.
- Nature (our biology), not nurture, drives entrepreneurial success.

And why do the most educated and trained CEOs get outrun by a college dropout?

Probing into these questions helped me discover why millions of books produce only a handful of successes. At the beginning of 2020, I finished my research and completed the first draft of this book. I had a number of successful entrepreneurial CEOs review it.

I was nervous.

This was the ultimate litmus test. Would they laugh? Call me just another wannabe? See nothing new?

Their feedback validated everything:

- "This is exactly what happened to me!"
- "I sure could've used this book when I started out! It would've saved me a lot of wasted time and emotional energy."
- "My wife couldn't put it down. She said it explained a lot, and she works in my business! She implemented three ideas from the book in 24 hours!"
- "My husband said he finally understood what I really went through when I started my company. It was humbling."

But what does this mean for you?

If you don't want to crash and burn or have to call in someone like me to save your ass, you're going to have to seriously overhaul your thinking. Are you willing to reevaluate what you know and unlearn a lot of the expert advice you've been following?

I'm not going to regurgitate the same old theories here; that's for other books. Instead, I'm going to bust myths, share where even I went wrong in my own entrepreneurial ventures (and I was wrong a *lot*!), and what I learned from it all.

Hang on tight. It's going to be a bumpy ride.

DEMOTIVATIONAL INTRODUCTION

> "The desire for safety stands against every great and noble enterprise."
>
> —Tacitus

So you want to be an entrepreneur.

Why not? Tons of books, motivational speeches, and online programs show you how to win. With so many experts ready to help, there's no reason to wait.

Like many entrepreneurs, you've read dozens of books on how to do it, and you're impatient to get started. It can be exciting. Just look at all those social media videos. Imagine you, with the love of your life, getting into a Lamborghini in front of your mansion on the way to your private jet.

OK. So let's get started!

But first, a small bit of advice . . . it's all bullshit.

But you already know this.

Let's back up a second. Whether you're just starting out, or you're several years down the road with a company you started, or you're an intrapreneur for a major firm, why did you want to be an entrepreneur?

- You've fallen for the hype.
- You're in a dead-end job trying to escape cubicle prison.
- You were recently fired.
- You were bored in your career and wanted to take on a risky new role in your company.
- You've just graduated and are living in your parents' basement.
- Your spouse abandoned you and took all the money.
- You are so tired of being cold, hungry, and poor that you're desperate to do anything.

No matter. They're all good enough reasons.

You see, I don't care about what made you buy this book or what gets you up in the morning.

What do I care about?

That first time, as you're skipping down that entrepreneurial yellow brick road to success, you slam into the Entrepreneur Wall of Despair (EWOD), fall down, crawl to a chair, lift yourself up, put your elbows on the table, lean over, head in hands, and let out a deep sigh because you now realize that being an entrepreneur totally sucks!

I care about how you look in the bathroom mirror as you wipe the blood and dirt off your face and in *that* moment say, "What the fuck was I thinking?"

I know exactly what you were thinking.

- You wanted the freedom to choose when and how long you worked each day (but then the eighteen-hour days screwed that up).
- You thought it'd be great not having a boss (until you found out you had a hundred bosses; they're called customers).

- Then you thought you'd have tons of money (until 80 percent evaporated on employees, distribution, marketing, sales, rent, utilities, lawyers, accountants, office staff, and production . . . and that's before you've even paid taxes!)

Oh, and when your costs grew too high, your banker gladly helped you fill that gap with loans on your house.

If that look of death in the mirror doesn't suck badly enough, watch what happens when your business assumptions get exposed as fantasies, or your expectations don't even come close to being achievable. How does it feel when your motivational "abundance mindset" gets obliterated by circumstances failing to cooperate with your precious well-laid plans?

OK, breathe.

I know that was hard to read. My editors told me to lighten up. They said motivational authors tend to inspire readers, pump them up, create a positive attitude, and encourage them.

But I told them you want to be an entrepreneur. So let's stop that crap.

You see, something special occurs in that EWOD body slam. A priceless secret hides there.

You will use this entrepreneurial secret to win.

Still serious about taking this journey?

Then let's talk.

AN UNCOMMON APPROACH

After MIT and Johns Hopkins, I banged around for twenty-five years doing leadership research, training over thirty thousand

CEOs, working with companies in over one hundred industries, and conducting expeditions around the world to study humans. I always dug deeper and climbed higher to disrupt the status quo and unearth fresh leadership insights even in the most unpleasant or dangerous conditions.

Why was I such a renegade?

In my defense, I had no adult supervision.

But when I started writing, I wasn't sure how to teach all this. Whenever I'm unsure what to do, I talk to smart people. Dov Baron had been developing an exciting model around what he calls the "Emotional Source Code." Being a researcher himself, he extensively reviewed my methods of teaching and said something unexpected.

"You're a mythbuster!"

A mythbuster? I thought about that for a moment. For years I'd exposed what's behind the high failure rates of management theories. Many CEOs drive higher sales and better organizational performance with these insights. But myths?

I ran this mythbuster idea by CEOs in my workshops, and they said Dov was right. One CEO said, "You not only exposed many commonly held myths to me but also used science to back it up."

So let's get at that entrepreneurial secret by busting some myths.

Stop looking for answers to the questions and start questioning the answers.

Learning the secret to entrepreneurship isn't going to be easy. We need to disrupt what you've already learned. I don't mean by being mildly critical, I mean by totally destroying all of it. You'll soon be asking yourself—and your employees—some very dangerous questions.

Are you ready?

If you're still reading, let's assume that's a "yes" (or your significant other said you have no choice).

If you're finishing up your entrepreneur classes and webinars and are still no better off, then this book is for you.

If you're sitting there depressed and humiliated from your latest entrepreneurial disaster or fearing another catastrophe looming, this book is for you.

If, however, none of this sounds like you but does sound like a friend, then buy them a copy now! *(Oops, shameless sales promotion.)*

But this book is *not* for you if you're a member of the lucky-sperm club with your parents' safety-net trust fund nicely protecting you from your mistakes.

You see, this book is for real entrepreneurs.

The ones with the dream who risk it all to make it happen. The ones who are willing to feel pain, sweat, fear, doubt, defeat, and humiliation.

You!

ENTREPRENEURSHIP: A CURSE, NOT A COURSE

What's the problem with thousands of books and courses out there showing you how to become a winning entrepreneur?

Nothing.

They all offer great ideas for getting it done. But why do only a handful of us succeed?

Because only a few of us realize this:

Entrepreneurs are cursed.

Why else would someone take such risks, remortgage their home, stress their family, and max out their credit cards?

Others have more common sense. They find a nice stable job.

And maybe you should too. Unless, of course, you're cursed. Here are two tests to find out if you're a real entrepreneur or just a pretender.

TEST #1: How Much Will You Risk?

Entrepreneurs are cursed to risk it all.

I started several small companies, and I set out to find real entrepreneurs to join me on the journey each time. One guy replied to an ad I posted. His résumé said he was an entrepreneur; in his interview he said he was an entrepreneur and understood the role he'd play as an entrepreneur. Then he uttered those dreaded words: "What's my salary?"

I explained we'd share in the profits. He said no, that he needed a paycheck of $100K. I said, "If I pay you $100K a year and it doesn't work out, what did you risk?"

He said his time.

Huh? I spend cold, hard cash on him and he just risks time? Time that he gets paid for!

Most self-proclaimed entrepreneurs have no idea what it means to be one.

A great example of taking entrepreneurial risk is Lou Tice, the late founder and chairman of The Pacific Institute, one of the most successful personal development institutes in the world. For over fifty years he created such popular concepts as "Mindset" and "Find Your Why." Today, the institute covers much of the globe, has educated millions, influences half of the Fortune 1000 companies, and evolved into a multimillion-dollar business.

How did he do it? With practically nothing. Having been a high school teacher and football coach (what he really wanted to be), Lou was faced with supporting a wife and six adopted kids, with only $1,000 in the bank.

How did Lou take such a risk?

When asked during speeches he'd say, "I didn't let the fear stop me. Yes, we risked a lot, but I figured I could always go back to teaching if it didn't work out. You see, if you let the fear of failure stop you from taking risks, you get nowhere in a hurry. History is littered with great ideas that weren't acted

on. And we didn't go from zero to millions in a few months. It was years of trying things—some worked, some didn't. But that didn't stop me. The reason I've been successful is that I was willing to try more things. The more you try, the more you succeed. If you only try one thing and it doesn't work, do you give up? Well, some people do, and then feel defeated for the rest of their lives. No, if you truly want to be successful, you try again, or try something different. You keep your mind open to opportunities, set your goals, and you figure out the 'how' on your way to your goal."

If you're like Lou, you're probably an entrepreneur.

TEST #2: Have You Been Called "Crazy"?

Entrepreneurs may be cursed due to their biology. OK, we're going to get politically incorrect here. Well, you're probably used to it by now if you read this far.

More than once I wondered if entrepreneurs are crazy. Why? Because I just didn't feel normal. And in doing research for this book, I found evidence that I'm not alone. People already think we're crazy for taking risks, but for about two-thirds of us it just might be caused by our biology.

To help you accept who you are, or at least understand your entrepreneurial colleagues better, research this yourself. Just google "is entrepreneurship a disorder" and you'll get thirty-five million hits (yes, read that again) on books and articles like:

- *Harvard Business Review*, "Entrepreneurship as Disease," by Jeff Stibel: *"I liken entrepreneurism to a disease. Having it myself, I am not always sure it is a good thing."*
- *Forbes*, "Why Entrepreneurs Need to Talk About

Their Mental Health," by Dan Murray-Serter: *"72% of entrepreneurs are affected by mental health issues . . . according to a study by the National Institute of Mental Health."*

- Or pick up a copy of Dr. John D. Gartner's book *The Hypomanic Edge: The Link Between (a Little) Craziness and (a Lot of) Success in America*: *"The idea that some entrepreneurs may be a little manic is hardly new. . . . Yet, until now, there has never been a serious suggestion that the talent for being an entrepreneur and mania, the genetically based psychiatric disorder, are actually linked."*

Now, I'm not saying that you have to be crazy to be an entrepreneur, only that it might help a lot! Clinical evidence even suggests that it might be useful to be a little nuts.

Here's my story. When I was sixty years old, I got diagnosed with ADHD. This explained why I was always criticized for my behavior. I had too many thoughts at one time, couldn't concentrate on one thing, shook my leg constantly so I could concentrate, had difficulty with attention to detail, was always starting new tasks before finishing old ones, organizational skills sucked, had too many priorities, was always losing or forgetting things, talked a lot, was extremely impatient, and took risks in physical activities, often with little or no regard for personal safety.

And those were my good features!

But although I had these problems, my ADHD gave me a superpower. I wasn't necessarily smarter but, like so many others, I felt as if my brain was operating faster than normal. Being able to generate a big-picture, global-thinking style facilitated making random connections between seemingly unrelated ideas or concepts. This allowed me to connect several

disparate scientific and historical findings into useful models such as:

- Using modern medical research to explain ancient leadership behaviors.
- Detecting the impact of biological leadership instincts on civilizations.
- Uncovering genetic dimensions that grow companies faster.
- Triggering our species' reflexes to induce faster cultural alignment and restructuring.
- Unhooking genetic warfare patterns to increase decisiveness and accountability.

This all resulted in evidence-based, strategic scientific methods I now use to train thousands of CEOs—improving corporate sales and organizational performance more than any other methods used.

Which raises the next question.

Is ADHD really a *dis*order, or is it an enhanced level of order? What if it's an *order* of the brain that helps create new companies, countries, sciences, technologies, and civilizations?

Well, I decided to check.

I wasn't alone. Bill Gates, Walt Disney, Richard Branson, Olympic gymnast Simone Biles, IKEA founder Ingvar Kamprad, award-winning actor Michelle Rodriguez, JetBlue founder David Neeleman, Jim Carrey, Howie Mandel, journalist Lisa Ling, Cisco Systems CEO John T. Chambers, Golden Globe winner Zooey Deschanel, actor Emma Watson, and many other brilliant leaders, researchers, and artists had the same condition (and Steve Jobs was suspected of having it). They all found ways to make ADHD work for them. Once they left their respective school systems, their ADHD transformed from a disorder into an advantage.

I was also not alone in pondering whether ADHD was a disorder or an advantage for an entrepreneur:

- In 2014, *Forbes* published the article "ADHD: The Entrepreneur's Superpower."
- Then, in 2015, *HuffPost* published "ADHD Can Be a CEO's Secret Superpower."
- In 2016, *Entrepreneur* magazine published "'Entrepreneurial ADHD' and How to Deal With It."

Although ADHD can be a powerful winning advantage, those of us with it know it can also wreak havoc on our lifestyle, love life, friendships, work, and the ability to parent. But articles like these reveal how top business leaders with ADHD exhibit many of the same unique characteristics. (I also want to pause here to say that you don't *need* to have ADHD to have these qualities and skills—you can develop them within yourself).[1]

- **Problem-Solving Abilities:** They easily see the big picture, have nonlinear thoughts, and perceive many different angles at once, helping them come up with solutions others may not.
- **Creativity:** Their world's a rainbow, not black and white. Their brain cannot focus on one thing for too long, so when they go back to problems later, they have ideas from the oddest of places and discover unconventional solutions.
- **Intuition:** Because they cannot easily focus, they are constantly aware of what's going on around them and can sense what will happen next—the good or bad.

- **Superior Idea Generation:** Creativity and intuition come together in new ideas for models, services, or products. One example is David Neeleman's e-ticket. After misplacing his airline tickets often, he created a paperless ticket system that changed the industry.
- **Risk-Taking Behaviors:** Because they have no time to reflect on an idea, they take risks and act impulsively, feeling they will forget about it, so they have to do it now!
- **High Energy:** The school system sees ADHD's high energy as a problem. But high energy in the workplace makes you more productive—so graduates deemed not likely to succeed often do very well in business.
- **Sense of Humor:** ADHDs make so many mistakes they learn to laugh at themselves and not take themselves so seriously. At the end of the day, they will laugh last.
- **Hyperfocus:** Many cope with not being able to focus on one thing for too long by having tools to focus. In a CNBC interview, Richard Branson said, "I have always lived my life by making lists: lists of people to call, lists of ideas, lists of companies to set up, and lists of people who can make things happen. Each day I work through these lists, and that sequence of calls propels me forward."

There you have it. If you think you have ADHD, fine. Now when people call you crazy for being an entrepreneur, just say, "Of course. Thanks for noticing."

OK. Crazy or not, let's get started.

We've got a road to travel together.

THE POWER OF LOSING

"The truth will set you free, but first it will piss you off!"

—Gloria Steinem

Tina stood up with the audience and applauded. The motivational speech so inspired her that, the next morning, she bolted to the airport with a better attitude than when she arrived. With renewed vigor to overcome obstacles and live a life of possibility, she couldn't wait to share it all back at the company she started a year ago.

At her office the next morning, something shifted. Still inspired by the conference, she felt uneasy as she passed the motivational posters and mission statement hanging in the hallway. She couldn't put her finger on it.

Arriving at her desk, she grabbed her empty coffee cup—the one with an inspirational quote on it—and headed to the kitchen. On the way she noticed a new self-help book on an employee's desk. Not unusual. A lot of staff kept up with the latest podcasts, TEDx talks, and bestselling books.

She stopped.

If we're so invested in the latest leadership trends, why

aren't we growing faster? She feared the morning's management meeting; growth was minimal, and margins were sinking.

She wasn't alone. Entrepreneurs spend billions annually on great motivational speakers, trainers, coaches, management consultants, books, and videos. But why are there so few winners?

What are we missing?

I got a clue after one of my speeches on ancient samurai leadership at an industry conference. A CEO walked up and asked, "Have you noticed a bestselling book's list of 'great companies' deteriorates a few years after publication? Maybe the best way to predict a failing company is to see who's in a bestselling book!" As he walked away laughing, I thought about how his comment opened up a very dark question.

Splitting a ride back to the airport, I shared this with a CEO. She said, "Can't argue with that. I've met many who ran great companies and hired all the top consultants and bestselling authors, but they still struggled; some failed."

"So what's an entrepreneur do to avoid that?" I said.

"I don't know. It's probably not in the books. How many business books are published annually?" she asked.

"About thirty-five thousand," I said.

"So why do we need thirty-five thousand new ones this year?" she said.

I loved the sarcasm. But I loved the logic even more. Could something deeper be stopping entrepreneurs from creating winning companies?

I was determined to find out, so I started doing some serious digging.

AUTOPSIES

Struggling with the question about why so many successful companies in bestselling books fail, I uncomfortably risked embarking into rare, unorthodox research. OK, I wasn't uncomfortable. You know by now I love doing rare, unorthodox research. But this required shifting my focus from studying successful companies . . . to studying the dead.

I began researching dead companies, and the smell got much worse. It wasn't just that many "great companies" failed rapidly after being in a bestselling book, it was that the management theories in the book failed!

What?

Yes. I researched published scholarly articles on management theory implementation; they reported failure rates from 70 to 90 percent. Just search Google Scholar on "management theory failure" and read the hits . . . all five million! (Well, don't read all five million. I want you to read this book.)

When I share this with CEO audiences, they are even more cynical. One said, "A multibillion-dollar management consulting industry with a failure rate that high? I'd be out of business in sixty days with that level of performance!"

Was I the only one disturbed by this failure-rate data? No. A lot of smarter people had been on this long before me. Failure-rate data had been exposed for decades by notable professors like Henry Mintzberg (McGill University) and Michael Beer[2] (Harvard Business School). Even recent books such as Phil Rosenzweig's *The Halo Effect* and Geoffrey Moore's *Zone to Win* reveal lists of carcasses.

I remember when Michael Beer presented his paper "Why Change Programs Don't Produce Change" at a top international conference of management consultants in New York City. I went there to try to learn something from the world's

top experts. When he told them that he had a hard time finding any bottom-line impact from their theories, what did they do?

Nothing. No one challenged his data.

And it got worse.

I studied Wall Street activity in mergers and acquisitions. There must be something working in the M&A industry, right? Joining companies to make them winners in their markets requires the best strategy, structure, systems, organizational change, and leadership talent. Surely they had figured out a foolproof formula to take a business and make it a winning success?

Well, I thought so. Don't read the 1.5 million articles published on M&A failure rates. I'll save you the time:

- ***Harvard Business Review:*** Study after study puts the failure rate of mergers and acquisitions somewhere between 70 percent and 90 percent.
- ***Forbes:*** Half of all M&A deals fail.
- **Wharton:** Failure rates of M&As are as high as 90 percent.
- **McKinsey:** M&As have 66–75 percent failure rates.
- **Accenture:** M&As have failure rates as high as 70 percent and, in some cases, even 90 percent.
- **CNN:** M&A failure rates are far north of 50 percent.
- **Bain:** M&As have a 70 percent failure rate.
- **Boston Consulting Group:** 70 percent of M&As fail to create meaningful shareholder value.

WTF?

The smartest people in the room can't succeed more often than that?

In a confused panic, I went back to the CEO community. And I didn't ask just a few. I asked thousands.

What did they say?

The failure data was right. They didn't see any notable results from management theories. The only consistent pattern I discovered was:

- CEOs are cynical about flavor-of-the-month theories.
- Managers are suspicious of consultants.
- Many employees just can't wait for their boss to read a new book!

So it's not the lack of management theories on how to win, it's that the theories themselves don't implement consistently. With research exposing the high failure rates, and the world's top management consultants unable to defend themselves, **what's an entrepreneur to do?**

I had no fucking idea.

So I did what any scientist would do in this situation. I banged my head on the desk . . . for months.

EPIPHANY

One night, leaning back in my chair, I glanced over all the research papers, books, and interview notes strewn across my desk in a horrible mess (nothing new about that; my staff will tell you my desk usually looks that way). What was I missing? There have always been successful entrepreneurs, but what are we not teaching about winning that would help create more successful entrepreneurs?

Then I had one of those blinding flashes of the obvious. Studying physics at MIT allowed me to see that breakthroughs

often occur not by finding new data, but by viewing the same data differently than others.

> "What we observe is not nature in itself, but nature exposed to our method of questioning."
>
> —Werner Heisenberg, theoretical physicist, pioneer of quantum mechanics

I figured the guy who could help me was Mark Levy, the brand coach behind the evolution of the most cutting-edge business brands, including Simon Sinek and his bestselling book, *Start with Why*. When Mark interviewed my entrepreneurial CEO clients to see why we were more successful than anyone else they had used, he discovered that my approach was different than the management consulting industry's. He said that I was really exposing the myth of how to be a winner. While everyone was preaching how to win by avoiding being a loser, I was doing the opposite. Instead of training executives on how to do what other winners do, I was calling bullshit.

Suddenly, it all became clear what was missing. So, let's pull back the curtain. What's the secret for becoming a winning entrepreneur?

Winning happens when you find your power in losing.

This is the opposite of what we're taught. "There are winners and losers. Be a winner. Losers look bad. They make dumb mistakes, wrong decisions, and do stupid things. Don't be a loser."

But I found the opposite is true for entrepreneurs. Losing powerfully is *your* secret for having a winning edge. Do not avoid losing. Embrace it.

We've devoted so much of our focus to winning (fifty thousand books have been published with "win" in the title) that the power of losing has been lost. Ignoring losing causes many entrepreneurs to throw in the towel way too early. Their journey—full of failure, humiliation, and mistakes—looks nothing like what they expected from the books and courses.

But the journey of losing is *exactly* what entrepreneurship looks like.

I flew out to another keynote speech and sat next to a successful entrepreneur CEO in the health care field. Seeing a great time to test what I thought, I asked her, "How many times did you lose before you developed such a winning business?"

I wasn't sure if she would reject my question or throw coffee in my face. But she was quiet. Then, leaning over, she said, "When I started this business, I had big dreams. I listened to a lot of motivational speakers and read a lot of those books you're talking about. They make it all sound so exciting. But what these experts fail to tell you is that underneath that fancy road to success is a dirty layer of false starts, failures, mistakes, and financial disasters muddied up in a sludge of blood and sweat."

She took a sip of coffee. "Whenever I win an industry award, I always thank my husband for tolerating the journey with me."

The secret of entrepreneurship?

Losers lose power, but winners lose powerfully.

I'm going to show you how.

But first . . .

How Did They Miss This?

How do consultants and experts miss that the secret to winning is, in fact, losing powerfully?

I couldn't figure it out. But after I did the desk head-banging thing again, it became obvious. They ignore it because they weren't there.

When authors show up to write books about a successful entrepreneur, they focus on what that entrepreneur did right. They weren't there earlier to observe the depths of fear, pain, and anguish every successful entrepreneur suffers through; to feel the agony, frustration, anger, sleepless nights, ruined relationships, and personal financial losses.

So, they missed the secret of "losing" because they weren't around when it happened. If they had been, they would have discovered what I saw in the data:

Failed companies don't just fail, they just fail to lose powerfully.

Let's Get Started

Time to learn how to lose powerfully.

I don't care whether you're selling real estate, online products, cosmetics, health care, pets, insurance, clothes, apps, pharma, technology, weight loss solutions, relationship advice, or whatever's hot these days. Or whether you're trying to pay the rent, afford your family's summer vacation, make the car payment, or, gasp, cover the kids' tuition.

It's time to focus on the one thing that scares the hell out of us: **losing in order to win.**

Yes, this is going to suck.

You're going to have to look where the experts have been

telling you *not* to. Time to face what they've been telling you to avoid.

Remember: "What doesn't kill you makes you stronger." Well, I thought this was true until I bought a T-shirt in Aspen that added, "Except for bears. Bears will kill you." But failure is not a bear. You'll be OK. Failure is your friend. And it's the best teacher.

Now, I'm not saying you should seek out failure for the sake of it or fail on purpose. The point is:

How you deal with failure determines whether you win or lose.

Let's jump into how we can lose powerfully.

NOTE:

To be fair, there are a few authors who do write candidly about their struggles, failures, losses, and experiences because they were there, and know how it all contributed to their successes. I recommend reading their books. Here are a few of them:

- *Reality-Based Leadership: Ditch the Drama, Restore Sanity to the Workplace, and Turn Excuses into Results* by Cy Wakeman, a personal friend who I learn so much from every minute we're together
- *Lean In: Women, Work, and the Will to Lead* by Sheryl Sandberg, the former Meta Platforms (Facebook) COO
- *Delivering Happiness: A Path to Profits, Passion, and Purpose* by Zappos CEO Tony Hsieh
- *The Power of Many: Values for Success in Business and in Life* by Meg Whitman, former president and CEO of eBay
- *Let My People Go Surfing: The Education of a Reluctant Businessman* by Patagonia founder and CEO Yvon Chouinard
- *Losing My Virginity: How I Survived, Had Fun, and Made a Fortune Doing Business My Way* by Richard Branson
- *Shoe Dog: A Memoir by the Creator of Nike* by Phil Knight, Nike founder. Bill Gates called it a "reminder of what the path to business success really looks like . . . a messy, perilous, and chaotic journey, riddled with mistakes, endless struggles, and sacrifice."

HOW TO LOSE POWERFULLY

RULE #1: GET BACK UP

> 七転八起
> "Fall down seven times, get up eight."
> —Japanese proverb

When you hit an EWOD (Entrepreneur Wall of Despair), you will fall. The reasons are endless—bad assumptions, unfortunate market shifts, supplier issues, employee problems, wrong data, the economy, the bank, and, well, you know the rest.

Always get back up.

This rule consistently appears in every great entrepreneur's history. Take great risks. Fall. Get back up. Then repeat, repeat, repeat.

Others never dare leap so far from safety to reach the other side.

But that's not you.

Entrepreneurs overcome losing with some sense of persistence and resiliency. They know where they want to go (and really want it) with a persistent drive; nothing will stop them, even financial loss. And in that loss, they get back up, take a

breath, and start again.

Lou Tice would tell the story of a friend he met as a thirteen-year-old on a junior football team. When his friend grew up, he started a very small construction company, expanded into building management, and now owns data-storage farms in multiple locations, in addition to other businesses. One day his friend tried to save a much-loved, high-end local department store from financial disaster. It failed in a couple years. He lost a fortune. His wife told him, "Don't do that again."

Did it stop him?

No. He picked himself up, dusted himself off, and continued to build his business empire.

Richard Branson also knows how to lose (it felt weird writing that). He's one of the top entrepreneurs in the world, but the first to admit when he fell. His first company in the magazine business didn't make money. He would've gone under without pivoting to records. Then his soda company, Virgin Cola, fizzled. His Virgin Cars couldn't rev up. Virgin Digital didn't download. His Virgin fashion companies weren't, well, fashionable. And, as of this writing, Virgin Orbit, sister company of Virgin Galactic, failed to achieve orbit, halting operations for the foreseeable future.

Even a successful venture like Virgin Atlantic Airlines almost crashed before it started. During the initial test flight with a rented Boeing 747, a flock of birds flew into an engine, causing so much damage that it threatened his certification as an airline.

Any one of Branson's losses could have derailed his success . . . if he'd allowed it to. But, as with all successful entrepreneurs, he kept getting back up.

And this is what sets real entrepreneurs apart from the rest.

What do the rest do?

They just stop.

Don't be like the rest. Be an entrepreneur.

Are you there now? In that valley of the shadow of death, engaging in the hopeless fight, drowning in a sea of despair? Are you totally spent, frightened, and ready to collapse? Are you tired of suffering and sacrificing so much?

Get back up and keep going.

Flawlessly executed plans, stirring speeches, and get-rich-quick theories-of-the-month don't birth winning entrepreneurs. They are birthed from the risks, pain, mistakes, and suffering that losing brings. This is not a journey for the weak.

Now get up.

RULE #2: ALWAYS BE PREPARED TO LEARN

> "I never lose. I either win or I learn."
>
> —Nelson Mandela

Tips like "make mistakes" and "fail fast" show up often in leadership books. For entrepreneurs, however, these themes exist deeper than just random moments for learning. Instead, they are a way of being, the source of all success. For some, an occasional mistake creates another motivational quote. But in the entrepreneur's world, it's the atmosphere we breathe. When companies learn how to fail fast, they establish team meetings to process what they learned. But an entrepreneur has to refinance their house, return the kids' holiday gifts, try to keep their marriage from falling apart, see if they can raise the credit limits on their Visa cards, cancel the family vacation, find food, attempt medication or, even more sadly, cope with addiction or thoughts of suicide.

Learning from mistakes and failing fast occurs differently for entrepreneurs.

Sam Walton was being interviewed by a reporter determined to uncover Sam's secret to success. Sam had built the most successful retail empire, Walmart, which today has become the world's largest company with $600 billion USD revenue[3] and 10,585 outlets in twenty-four countries. It's also the world's largest private employer with 2.2 million employees.

Sam told the reporter he made a lot of mistakes in growing Walmart. But the reporter was relentless. Determined to find Sam's real answer to success, he kept badgering Sam on how he did it. But Sam just kept telling the reporter that he made a lot of mistakes. Seeing the reporter getting frustrated, Sam finally admitted that his success came from experience. Relieved that he was finally making progress, the reporter asked, "How did you get that experience?" Sam replied, "I keep telling you. I made a *lot* of mistakes!"

The more I researched this idea, the more I realized that learning from losing requires the art of optimism.

The research of Dr. Martin Seligman from the University of Pennsylvania confirms why it's OK to be optimistic even if everyone says you're crazy to keep going. The Pacific Institute CEO, Mark Panciera, says it's one of the factors that make their courses so successful. "Dr. Seligman's work on both optimism and pessimism revealed that people with an optimist outlook—not pie-in-the-sky wishful thinking, but a belief system that functions on knowing that things will work out—succeed far more often than pessimists. You see, pessimists color their entire world with doom and gloom. If something bad happens, then it's personal (I caused it), permanent (it'll never change), and pervasive (it'll undermine everything I try to do). The optimist takes responsibility for their part, knows that the situation will pass, and limits the effect to that one

small area of the situation. For the optimist, failure becomes a learning experience. And, once the lesson is learned, it's filed away in the subconscious, a memory to be accessed when a similar situation arises in the future."

To see how this works, let's investigate the famous failure-machine—Michael Jordan. What? Blasphemy! Michael is an inspirational winner, not a failure!

I agree. But peek behind the curtain and he himself reveals the secret to being a winner:

"I've failed over and over and over again in my life, and that is why I succeed. Some people want it to happen, some wish it would happen, others make it happen. I can accept failure; everyone fails at something. But I can't accept not trying. If you're trying to achieve, there will be roadblocks. I've had them; everybody has had them. But obstacles don't have to stop you. If you run into a wall, don't turn around and give up. Figure out how to climb it, go through it, or work around it."

What did he mean when he said he'd failed?

- He missed more than 9,000 shots.
- He lost almost 300 games.
- He missed 26 game-winning shots!

And that all happened after he was cut from his high school varsity basketball team! He failed *more* than he succeeded. And he learned every time.

Everyone fails. It's the people who learn the most from their failures who succeed. Mark Manson, in his book *The Subtle Art of Not Giving a F*ck*, captures the idea perfectly:

"Improvement at anything is based on thousands of tiny failures, and the magnitude of your success is based on how many times you've failed at something."[4]

So always be prepared to fail.

Losing isn't a momentary glitch. It's the foundation of winning.

RULE #3: SEIZE THE MOMENT

OK. Take a deep breath. Look back at your life.

How many times have you been on that "road to success" and tripped? Remember that moment we talked about earlier? That painful EWOD moment when you sit down, put your head in your hands, lean over with your elbows on the table, and with a deep sigh realize that being an entrepreneur totally sucks?

Good. Because as you lift yourself up, spit dirt out of your mouth (hard to forget that taste), feel your face numb from hitting the ground, gasp as that last sucker-punch of failed expectations knocks the air out of your lungs, and wonder why anyone would want to be an entrepreneur, something "special" happens.

Contrary to what all the motivational experts say, seize that moment. Do *not* run away.

- Do *not* pull out your inspirational quotes.
- Do *not* start your positive-thinking exercises.
- Do *not* put on your brain wave music.
- Do *not* start chanting.
- Do *not* deny where you are.

Instead, I want you to stay right there. Stay in *that* moment and really focus on it.

Why?

Because *that's* the moment you become an entrepreneur.

Seize it.

Don't run. Explore. What did you miss? Is this a common pattern? What can you learn? What could you have done differently?

That EWOD is the moment of building strength. What you do at that moment separates you from the rest. It separates

you from the wannabes, the complainers, the braggarts, the blamers, the haters, and the excuse-makers.

That moment of losing is when you become a *real* entrepreneur. Self-proclaimed experts don't talk about those depressing, demotivating, brutal falls. But the hairy reality is you *need* to experience them.

Now that you know how to lose powerfully, what can stop you? That's next. But first let's see how all this plays out in the real world.

Case Study: Dan Lok

Nobody saved Dan Lok. Now a serial entrepreneur and bestselling author, when Dan hears people tell him he has the Midas touch—and they tell him this often—he can't help but laugh. He tells them, "You should have met me years ago when everything I touched turned to shit. Everything I planned for was just a disaster. I failed at thirteen businesses before having my first success."

When Dan was fourteen years old, he and his parents emigrated from China to Canada. The family had no money and no connections, and Dan didn't speak a word of English. Dan's parents divorced two years later. His father returned to Hong Kong, where he started a company that went bankrupt (thanks to his business partner running off with all the money). The cash he had been sending to Dan and his mother dried up.

No amount of motivational quotes could pull a young kid out of this pit of despair. "My dad couldn't support my mom and me anymore," Dan recalls, "so I had to stop being a boy and grow up. I knew that if I wanted to provide for my mom, I couldn't just be a minimum wage worker in somebody else's business. I had to be mature and start my own. Over the next few years, I was like a young hustler, trying a bunch of different things to see what would stick."

Sounds like a good plan, but it didn't work. Dan's first

venture was to partner with a couple of high school buddies and mow lawns for people in their neighborhood. They did OK—until winter came, then it sucked. While still in school, his next venture was stocking vending machines, but that wore thin. Then he fixed people's computers and did food deliveries, but just like everything else he tried, he lost interest or they ended in failure. Dan and his mom fell deeper into debt, living on meals of day-old bread from a nearby bakery and overripe fruits and vegetables from the grocery store's bargain bin. Welcome to suffering and sacrifice.

But then Dan met his first mentor, Allan Jacks, who ran one of the most successful financial settlement companies in Canada. One day, Jacks asked Dan a question he never forgot—a question that introduced Dan to the concept of destruction of motivation. "What do you think is the most common quality among successful entrepreneurs?"

Dan rolled out the typical responses. Talent? Intelligence? Teamwork? Vision? Humility? Execution? Leadership?

Jacks replied that while those were all important qualities, none was number one. In his opinion, the number one quality of a successful entrepreneur is *the ability to endure pain for a long period of time*. Here was a real entrepreneur.

"And it is so true," Dan says. "Sometimes people ask me what kept me going after all those failed businesses, and I always wish I could say that it was my determination and drive. But the truth is that I was young and naïve, and I didn't know what I didn't know. I didn't know I was *supposed* to quit."

When Dan was in his early twenties, he went to work with Jacks. Over a twelve-month period, he learned all about marketing, sales, and how to communicate with people. Dan refers to that period as his "million-dollar year" because of the rich education he received working alongside his mentor. He took what he learned and started a one-man advertising agency, writing ads and marketing materials for entrepreneurs and

business owners. And this time, it worked. Dan made good money for such a young man, almost $10,000 a month. He was able to pay off the debts he had racked up, and he could finally provide for himself and his mom.

But Dan's entrepreneurial journey wasn't over yet. There was one thing that continued to bug Dan, and it was his inability to communicate orally. Remember, when he first arrived in Canada, he couldn't speak anything but Chinese, and he was one of the only Chinese kids at his school. Dan did his best to be invisible by always sitting at the back of the classroom and never volunteering an answer during class discussions. Despite his best efforts to fly under the radar, he was bullied and even beaten up a few times. As an adult, his lack of fluency with the English language naturally affected his confidence as an entrepreneur.

"I remember once—I think it was grade eleven—when I had to deliver a speech in English class and I was so terrified I hid in the bathroom," Dan says. "I couldn't do it. Later on, when I got into business, I knew I had to get a handle on this speaking thing because it was holding me back. So I joined Toastmasters to help improve my English."

Dan showed up at the Toastmasters meetings every single week. He practiced delivering all kinds of speeches and took in the constructive criticism the other participants wrote on little slips of paper. At first there was a lot of feedback and suggestions for how he could improve, but after six months Dan noticed that the notes from his peers were getting shorter and shorter.

"Dan, you are amazing!"

"That was awesome!"

"Incredible presentation!"

"You are a natural at this!"

"Me? A natural?" Dan laughs. "There was nothing natural about it!"

But over time, Dan started to fall in love with sharing his story and inspiring people through public speaking. He began studying the great motivational speakers of the day—Tony Robbins, Zig Ziglar, and Brian Tracy, especially. Sometimes he would even go see them live, and he'd sit in the audience and think how cool it would be to do what they did. But deep down he knew there was no way that was ever going to happen. First of all, he was too young. Second of all, he was Chinese.

"There were no Chinese people in the American public speaking world," Dan says. "They did not exist. Not even my mother believed I could do it. But it didn't matter. Even though I never expected to be paid to speak about my entrepreneurial journey publicly, it was my dream. I just kept doing it. The more speaking I did, the better I got."

When Dan was in his mid-twenties, he spoke at a workshop, selling his internet marketing program to entrepreneurs. He was given the worst possible spot in the speaker lineup—dead last at the end of a long day of presentations. As he was taking the stage, half of the audience was leaving. Dan took a deep breath and delivered his speech anyway. He didn't sell a single program that afternoon, but he was not discouraged. He knew there was nowhere to go but up.

Dan kept refining and delivering his speeches, and eventually he started making sales—lots of them. By the time he was twenty-six, he was traveling North America making hundreds of thousands of dollars a year as a professional sales speaker. When most of his peers were happy to have 10 percent of the room buy their offers, Dan was consistently converting 25 to 40 percent of attendees. One day, he outsold all six other speakers combined.

"And again, I'm hearing people tell me, 'You are so good, you're a natural,'" Dan says. "Of course, they don't know the hard work I put into this. To go from being the kid who never put up his hand, the kid who had no friends, who couldn't

speak a word of English, to this? Now I'm writing books, I'm traveling the world and speaking. I'm giving TEDx talks, and I'm even going to be sharing the stage with Tony Robbins in a few weeks. Not in a million years could I have imagined I'd be doing this for a living. But it goes to show the power of sticking with your goals, focusing on what you want, putting all your effort behind it, *and enduring pain for a long period of time.*"

MANAGEMENT MYTHS STOPPING YOU FROM LOSING POWERFULLY

How many times have you seen an entrepreneur get slammed by consultants for how their business model and strategy are all wrong? Or hear industry experts say they'll never make it?

I have. A lot.

But what do the experts and consultants do when this start-up rises to dominate the industry? They shut up. Some even write books on how these entrepreneurs became great!

Many times entrepreneurs don't follow experts. Their intuition drives them to challenge industry best practices and expose current industry knowledge as management myths.

A management myth is real until it's debunked and exposed.

What management myths sabotage you so that you don't lose powerfully?

Glad you asked . . .

DEBUNKED MANAGEMENT MYTH #1: PEOPLE FOLLOW YOU

On October 5, 2011, Steve Jobs died. The world mourned the loss of a genius. His iconic impact and the rise of Apple under his legendary guidance were epic achievements. Millions have an Apple product or have been affected by their intuitive approach to enhancing the user experience with technology.

But after his death, many authors wrote books about Steve Jobs.

They said he was an asshole.

Steve was unpleasant to work with. They describe how he was always shouting down colleagues and was visibly impatient, dismissive of others' contributions, rude, ruthless, and self-absorbed. He harassed and humiliated his staff and was often raging.

Which raises an interesting question. How does a guy who violates what's taught in our business schools and promoted in our bestselling books create the most powerful company in the world?

It gets worse. I discovered that Steve was not alone. As I dug further, I found other leaders were exposed as assholes in articles such as *The Washington Post*'s "Do jerks make better leaders?"[5]

Author Geoffrey Nunberg says, "If you just start ticking off names, it sure seems to help. . . . Michael Eisner, Larry Ellison, Martha Stewart, Meg Whitman, Sam Zell, Carly Fiorina, Bob Nardelli, 'Chainsaw Al' Dunlap, Richard Fuld, Mark Hurd, Jeffrey Skilling."

I even found out that General Patton and Mother Teresa were assholes.

OMG, Mother Teresa was an asshole?

What's going on? Why are people following leaders who are assholes?

The question consumed me.

But I was even more surprised that no one else was asking this question.

The Paradox

We are taught that in order to win, leaders must have followers. So all business schools, management trainings, and coaches tell us to attract and lead followers by doing things like:

1. Showing empathy
2. Being a good listener
3. Embracing change
4. Developing a mission or vision
5. Developing followers
6. Communicating
7. Continuing your education
8. Creating trust
9. Articulating clear goals and ensuring you and your team have clear roles
10. Being open to new ideas
11. Establishing accountability

We are told that followers follow the leaders who do these things well.

But, if this is true, why do people also follow assholes who violate many of these leadership qualities?

What are we missing in leadership education?

I found the answer during a Himalayan expedition. Studying remote and ancient cultures helps me discover new leadership methods I can use to help grow companies faster. Expeditionary travel sounds exotic, glamorous, and romantic, but only to people who've never done it. People think I'm like

Indiana Jones, but those who travel with me to remote regions in Asia and Africa know the truth. The experience is more like parasites, food poisoning, weird insect bites, weeks without a bath, near-death experiences, rashes, vomiting, no electricity, no toilet paper (sometimes dawning on you after you poop in a hole you just dug yourself), wondering whether the water you just drank was sanitized enough (which might magnify the previous experience), and so on. Then of course there's the exhaustion and altitude sickness.

None of this is in the fancy travel brochures.

This expedition was to a place many considered a lost civilization: Bhutan. Since it developed in isolation for many centuries, few countries knew Bhutan existed, and it appeared on very few maps until the 1770s, when it came to the attention of Europeans.

Studying lost civilizations developing in isolation is a cool way of figuring out which leadership instincts are encoded in our biology. If these civilizations are running businesses like you are, those instincts are probably genetic. I like teaching biologically based leadership methods because they work better than trendy management theories.

The government of Bhutan, one of the hardest countries in the world to enter, let only about forty of us in. A dozen of us were part of an expeditionary team. I wasn't going on a bus tour. This was a trek for weeks into remote mountains to visit cultures uncontaminated by Western thought.

When I entered Bhutan, the first thing I noticed was that lost civilizations aren't really lost. I find that they seem to know exactly where they are. And when we showed up, they didn't really thank us for "finding" them.

Crossing multiple Himalayan passes allowed me to visit exquisite valleys, enter unusual temples, and befriend curious villagers who often flock out to see these "strange" visitors. I fell in love with the Bhutanese, but it took a couple weeks for

me to get used to their practice of penis worship. Yes. You read that correctly. Penis worship. I remember finding out about this and laughing when I was eight years old, reading a Ripley's Believe It or Not! comic in a Bazooka bubble gum wrapper. You can Wiki it.

But I learned something remarkable about leadership at the end of this expedition. Not from the Bhutanese but from the Americans on my team.

We had a terrific anthropologist leading our expedition. He did a great job keeping us together, motivated, and moving ahead even when it was challenging. After many weeks of sleeping in tents, trekking the Himalayas, pooping in the woods, and eating yak meat, we were finally reaching the end of the expedition.

Success, right?

Not quite. Something strange happened.

We started disintegrating as a team. Instead of being a cohesive, collaborative group, we started splitting up into cliques and complaining about everything. "Why is my tent over there?" "How come it's taking so long to get hot water?" "Who does he think he is?" "They're getting on my nerves!"

I later discovered that teams often disintegrate at the end of expeditions. When I wrote *High Altitude Leadership* with one of the top climbers in the world, Chris Warner, his stories of expeditions on life-threatening peaks made our book read like a novel. He confirmed that a lot of expeditions fail at the end, not the beginning. And he should know. If you climb Everest, the bodies of the people you step over or around usually died when they were on the way down, not up.

But what happened to us in Bhutan?

We had a great leader, so why did we stop following him and degrade so fast?

Further research uncovered something remarkable.

Demystifying

"I would rather discover one true cause than gain the kingdom of Persia."

—Democritus

Like many expeditions, we failed at the end because we didn't have another mountain pass on the horizon. We were never really following our leader. We were following something bigger—the possibility to conquer a dramatic challenge ahead. Our leader was only presenting that challenge to us and inspiring us to achieve it.

But doesn't our company mission, vision, or "why" statement create that drama?

No. This is something deeper.

Legendary leaders throughout history knew that winning requires creating a drama ahead that inspires people—a challenge so formidable that followers believe they *need* each other in order to achieve it, and they must be inspired to do two things we never teach in management training:

Suffer and sacrifice together.

We call this a Winning Saga. I stole it from the Vikings. And what a great discovery they made. People follow the story—the drama the leader represents. How else do you get people to leave their safe village and climb aboard your boat? Do you promise them an enjoyable, fun cruise? Do you hang motivational posters on the deck of the ship?

No.

You present a Winning Saga. The Vikings conjured up stories of gods, kings, and heroes. The result? They were inspired to get on those boats bound for dangerous waters even though they knew many of them would likely die. Why? Because if

they died, others would write poems and sing songs about their heroic feats, and they would hear them singing from Valhalla.

So, our Bhutan expedition failed at the end because there was no future drama. We didn't have a story for what was ahead. We didn't have a new challenge with which to replace a Himalayan pass.

**Followers don't follow leaders.
They follow the Winning Saga the
leader represents.**

But isn't this the opposite of what the experts have been telling us? Aren't we supposed to get rid of drama?

Well, these experts haven't cracked open a medical journal. If they did, they'd learn that having no drama in life is pathological. People without drama get physically ill, and some of them die. This explains everything from the research on healing rates to the early deaths of retirees to soldier deaths in prisoner-of-war camps for no identifiable medical reason.

So, do the opposite of what they've been teaching you:

Don't get rid of drama. Give it to them!

You don't get people on board your ship because you're empathetic, humble, trustworthy, accountable, clear, and a good communicator. Those are all nice qualities and great to have. But people follow you because of what you're up to: What does winning mean? How and where are we going to do it? Give your employees a drama—your strategic winning drama.

Look at all the great leaders whose followers won in spite of the most impossible odds. Each time, you'll find people following a story, a possibility that the leader created. Think about Steve Jobs again. People weren't following him. They were following his intention: "We're here to put a dent in the universe."

They knew that if they followed him, they could elegantly violate the status quo! So they lined up to get on *his* ship—and so did the customers!

Other examples of Winning Sagas created by entrepreneurial companies when they were starting out include:

- 3M: Solve unsolved problems innovatively
- HP: Technical contributions for the advancement of humanity
- Mary Kay: Give unlimited opportunity to women
- Ritz Carlton: Ladies and Gentlemen serving Ladies and Gentlemen
- Mercedes: The best-engineered car in the world
- Ford (1900s): Democratize the automobile
- Komatsu: Encircle Caterpillar
- Lexus: Beat Benz
- Stanford (1940s): Become the Harvard of the West
- Coke: Put Coke within "arm's reach of desire"
- Nike: Experience emotions of competition, winning, and crushing competitors.
- Walmart: Give ordinary folks the chance to buy the same things as rich people.
- FedEx: Beat the UPS "brown shirts" with our red, white, and blue trucks!
- Zappos: Let There Be Shoes
- Amazon: Be Earth's most customer-centric company where people can find and discover anything they might want to buy online.
- Uber: Make transportation as reliable as running water, everywhere, for everyone.

Having a Winning Saga for your team to follow is not new. Research at The Pacific Institute found that drive and

motivation to move forward occur when we internalize our goal and form a picture of the finish line in our minds. The huge gap between where we are and where we want to be engages our creative subconscious (Lou Tice's term) that then provides the energy, ideas, and focus to get us to the goal line.

But when you get closer to the goal, shouldn't you feel great that you're going to be successful?

No.

This is when the leader should become nervous, because something surprising happens. The more the "before and after" pictures become similar, the less energy, focus, and motivation occur. The closer you get to achieving your Winning Saga, the more your people will lose drive and energy, and oftentimes, never reach the goal.

The solution? Set another goal, a new Winning Saga, further out. When you do that, energy, drive, and ideas reboot, and you're off to the races once again. Continuously reset your goals farther out so as you reach your original goal, you'll have the energy you need to continue.

You can even use this method personally. One CEO went through the worst divorce with the most malpractice committed that twelve reviewing attorneys had ever seen. After his wife abandoned him, he filed for divorce. His ex-wife fired attorneys until she found an infamous lawyer known for unethical manipulations and damaging children, sending many kids to child psychologists in order to win. Her lawyer taught her how to lie under oath and hold the kids hostage so she could get 120 percent of his assets (not 50 percent), get years of alimony, collapse his companies, force a tax lien on him from HER assets, stick him with the kids' education and medical expenses even though she stole the kids' educational funds, and reward herself with breast implants. The CEO complied in order to protect his kids from further abuse.

What kept him going? His Winning Saga: Save the children

of the village from an evil queen of darkness. So every morning he got up, picked up his battered shield and bloody sword, and went back into battle—for over ten years.

The CEO lost powerfully and won. He got full custody, his kids graduated from fine institutions, and they are now on to successful careers. He started a new business, a lot wiser and stronger.

Ready to implement?

How to Lose Powerfully Now That You Know Your Followers Don't Follow You

Your followers are sure as hell not going to follow you just because you're a nice person. You better have a Winning Saga. In creating that for companies over twenty years, I found these tips helpful. Use them to create your Winning Saga:

1. **Define what winning means.** Understand what winning means before you create the strategy for how to do it.
2. **Develop your winning strategy.** Remember that it's more about intuition and instinct than analysis; it's not about doing a SWOT analysis. How did a lot of small entrepreneurial companies like Southwest Airlines, Zappos, Virgin, and Apple outmaneuver big corporations? Ignore the experts and follow your intuition to outsmart the enemy.
3. **Create your Winning Saga** from your winning strategy. This then allows the creation of Critical Success Factors (those few factors necessary and sufficient for you to achieve your Winning Saga; we typically limit our clients to only five of these).

4. **Test and tune** that Winning Saga with your employees. Feedback is useful as you craft it.
5. **Lead** from that Winning Saga. Lead with this story, not with yourself.
6. **Align.** Make sure your executive team aligns with the Winning Saga and leads with it too, not themselves. If they're unclear, educate them in how to communicate the story to their respective teams.
7. **Extend.** Explore how this Winning Saga can be expressed in your products, service offerings, or branding.

If the Winning Saga can be applied to customers too, use it in your PR. If not, create a version where the public can align with it. Don't forget that customers can also be inspired to follow the story your products and services represent. That's how you create fans.

Case Study: Jeromy Stallings

Jeromy is the founder of Ninthlink, a multipurpose marketing and digital design firm in San Diego whose mission is to change our consumption habits by guiding consumers to companies that share their commitment to "product quality, employee well-being, and positive social and environmental change."

It's working. Clients include Quicken, Google, Jacuzzi, Qualcomm, Adidas, Acura, and Seiko, to name a few.

When I asked Jeromy which business "rules" he'd personally discovered were total BS, he didn't hesitate: the myth that followers follow leaders.

"People follow your story," he said. "Your leadership must start from a place of truth about why the company exists in the first place, even though this question might cause the company to be completely dismantled."

Why do you believe your product matters to the consumer? Why do you think you matter?

When an entrepreneur thinks about why the business they are running matters to the world and matters to them, it helps them win in the marketplace.

In realizing the power of the "why a company does what it does" story, Jeromy has played a huge role in the success of many businesses. But when they don't do this, they end up "making products and selling to consumers based on a whole statement of bullshit," he finds.

"By focusing on the 'why' and 'the right thing' and then only doing the stuff that supports that, we get a whole shift in perspective, which ultimately leads to better execution," Jeromy says. "I find this to be a really constructive way of leading, and I also find that the people come away feeling a lot more purposeful about what they are doing. They gain strength and confidence because everything's finally in alignment. They will work tirelessly from then on because they understand the purpose and everything makes sense."

Jeromy also walks the talk in his own business ventures. One such venture, founded with a former president of an American stock exchange company and a former Harvard professor who is now director of research at Scripps, focused on applying nicotinamide adenine dinucleotide (NAD) in nutrition for cellular health.

The product Jeromy and his partners came up with ticked every box it needed to in order to be a market leader. They'd done their research when it came to their competitors and ideal consumer, orchestrated a killer marketing campaign, and followed what they thought would be viable.

It didn't work.

"And that's because we forgot to do what we're talking about right now," he says, "which is to ask ourselves why we were making these products for ourselves in the first place.

Once we finally got around to asking that question, it entirely tore down the integrity of what we were doing. We had a total meltdown. It was hard to admit that nine months previous we thought we had this all figured out, yet we were so wrong."

Jeromy and his team started over. "We needed to show people the authentic story of what it really looks like to take this product," he says. "So we decided to get in front of our own cameras and take pictures of our own lifestyle and that of our families. We did it that way because we had lost our voice along the way. The product had lost its original, authentic notion, its purpose. No one aspired to any of it because it's all just based on bullshit fill-in-the-blank templates."

Jeromy's epiphany reinforced the importance of developing a strategic drama, a Winning Saga, which helped him to not only become a good leader but also guide his clients to peak performance.

Case Study: Marx Acosta-Rubio

Sometimes having a Winning Saga transforms both your leadership style and you personally. CEO Marx Acosta-Rubio experienced this.

When I met Marx, I was impressed with his energy and strategic focus but learned that he himself had a history of EWODs. Marx was born in Caracas, Venezuela; migrated to the US in 1977 unable to speak English; and was being raised by a single mom. He was always in trouble at school, got Ds and Fs, and flunked fifth grade. His mom sent him back to live in Venezuela during tenth grade because she could not afford to feed him.

By the time Marx got back, there wasn't much hope for him. He smoked three packs of cigarettes a day, woke up with a beer, and went to sleep with a whiskey. He had been in shootouts and caused havoc wherever he went.

But one day Marx had his entrepreneurial epiphany.

By the time he was twenty-eight, he was making $250,000 selling for an organization, which then fired him after three and a half years. He got fired because the owner of the company lacked integrity and Marx let him know it.

By this time, he owned a home and had a beautiful wife and one-year-old baby boy but zero money in the bank. In fact, he was still $35,000 in debt.

So as soon as he got home, he told his wife he was fired, and she quickly took the kids to Grandma's, got a business license, and made Marx get on the phone the very next day.

First year he sold $800,000 on the phone. By age thirty-one he had $1 million in cash in the bank. By thirty-seven he had over $10 million in cash in the bank.

Then EWOD. By thirty-eight he had zero dollars in cash in the bank, and by thirty-nine he had *negative* $2 million.

After wanting to give up and asking himself "why bother?" he seized that EWOD moment and built his business back up—only this time faster and smarter.

Now, at forty-eight, he is worth more (in CASH) than he ever was and owns or has part ownership in thirteen companies.

But by losing powerfully, Marx learned to create his own Winning Saga, which propelled his leadership success. In his early twenties, he thought leadership was all about how charismatic, flamboyant, and verbose you could be.

"And so that's how I led," he says. "I thought I was Midas and my stuff didn't stink. But when you become the issue, the essence, you're just another icon for the company. You inhibit the growth of other people. I later realized that I needed a personal Winning Saga that was all about helping other people."

Marx evolved this Winning Saga and focused on how he could help others by first developing the people working in his company. He stopped worrying so much about whether or not they'd stay with him. He said it was like striking gold.

"When you help people grow, they're more likely to follow you. You're a leader when you think about *what you can contribute*. That's what leadership means to me."

When Marx took on the story of helping and contributing to his people, it made *the* difference. His people stopped following him and began following the story he represented. They believed in helping themselves personally grow, and in helping others.

What was the result?

His company, OneStop, became a highly successful Inc. 500 company.

DEBUNKED MANAGEMENT MYTH #2: WORK YOUR PLAN

> "I may lose a battle but I will never lose a minute."
>
> —Napoleon Bonaparte

Matt Eversmann looks down out of the Black Hawk chopper and sees a body already on the ground. Their plan for a simple extraction has gone to shit and he's not even down yet. Matt doesn't know it, but he's in the middle of what will later be known as one of the most epic military planning failures in modern history, the Battle of Mogadishu, later to be immortalized in the bestselling book and hit movie *Black Hawk Down*.

If you believe what they teach you—that if you plan hard enough and execute that plan, you'll be successful—then don't talk to Matt. He knows better. This is why I wanted to work with him—to gain an unparalleled insight into the myth of planning.

I met Matt after he left the military. He knew about my leadership research and we hit it off right away, sharing our

experiences and insights. I always learned a lot getting together with Matt. He likes Italian wine. We went through a lot of Italian wine.

What I learned is that we teach planning all wrong. We tell entrepreneurs how to make a plan and then execute it with proper project management techniques. We tell them that success occurs when you have a great plan and follow through. It's Management 101. Who can argue with the logic?

I can.

It doesn't work.

Demystifying

I know what you're thinking. All the experts tell you to make a plan, and now here I am telling you to destroy it! You think I'm crazy? The only thing crazier than that is that you keep reading this book!

Look, I'm not saying the experts are wrong. Sure, you need a plan and should have one. There are a lot of good courses out there on how to plan effectively. Plans help you hold yourself and others accountable, schedule resources, meet deadlines, and map out the critical path to key strategic goals.

But working with Matt helped me realize that, while planning is important, it's not the same as execution.

During execution, things go wrong.

Speaking to the military—where I heard firsthand from those who've literally bet their life on plans—helped fast-track my understanding of *why* plans don't work. When my methods eventually made their way to the Pentagon, they asked me to tour military operations as a guest of the Secretary of Defense and the Joint Chiefs of Staff. What a great privilege! Originally, I turned them down. I didn't have the time. But then they told me I was going to see what CNN was not allowed to see and I

had permission to ask anybody anything I wanted at any time. What an incredible learning laboratory experience for me! I accepted immediately. And learned a lot!

Later I ended up facilitating sessions that transformed naval fleet readiness. And then I developed a leadership training program for corporate executive teams with the former dean of the Army War College.

With each event I gained a deeper insight into planning—or, at least, its inadequacy.

What I learned is:

No plan survives impact with reality.

Why? Because, as Matt told me while I was researching his "Black Hawk Down" experience, "The enemy has a vote, and they may vote no."

Your enemy may be competitors, suppliers, customers, technology, globalization, regulations, or sociopolitical shifts. These, along with unpredicted circumstances and bad assumptions, pretty much ensure your plan may fail to launch. Yes, you need a plan, but your enemies may not agree.

Lou Tice researched this over fifty years ago at The Pacific Institute. He rarely used the word *no* because he wanted people to think *yes* when challenges came up. When he spoke to states' superior court justices he said, "I sat there and listened to speaker after speaker moan and groan about all that was wrong and no way of fixing anything. Before I got up to speak, I decided to abandon what I was going to tell them. After my introduction, my first words to the group were 'The answer to your problems is *yes*.' Then I went on to teach them about how the mind interprets words and beliefs, and that they were allowing themselves to be stopped from finding solutions, trapping themselves with their own words."

But when it came to planning? He used the word *NO.*

"Make your plan, then work your plan? NO!" Lou was not a fan of plans. Rigid plans are a symptom of a fixed mindset. "You need to leave room for the unexpected. Keep the goal in mind, but don't lock onto how you are going to get there. A growth mindset leaves you ready to handle what you can't see coming at the start. Rarely is there a straight line, without interruptions, between beginning and ending. The path jogs right and left, up and down, and sometimes needs to go backwards a bit before springing forward. It's the end result you need to keep in mind."

Foolproof plans can't predict evolving market landscapes, competitive shifts, changing customer buying priorities, supply chain disruptions, technology impacts, talent issues, employee problems, or even whether you were just too optimistic. That's why your plan to create an amazing organization, hire the best talent, build a remarkable product that customers love, and make a difference in the world probably won't work.

It happens. Your company doesn't grow like the motivational keynote speaker told you it would, or your product issues become hard to fix, or the market won't respond like you thought it would, or your organizational culture degrades as turnover picks up, or people start doubting the dream as your competition looms greater and customer losses mount. Then you start questioning whether you're good enough to do this or just an imposter.

Relax. Many bankrupt companies had large binders of plans and hired the top planning professionals.

Yet some of the most successful companies had only a short document. My co-author on the book *High Altitude Leadership*, Chris Warner, launched one of the most successful climbing gyms and expedition companies in the country. His plan? Written on toilet paper with a CEO client he was stuck with in a tent on the side of a mountain for many days during a storm.

I found this out personally. We began growing companies two to three times faster when we threw out their planning binders and changed how they did strategic planning. We showed them that their plans were tactical, not strategic; then engaged their intuition for outmaneuvering industry threats. But the magic invoking the key to successful execution: adaptation.

How to Lose Powerfully Now That You Know Your Plans Won't Work

As the universe fails to meet your expectations, or the plan on the whiteboard doesn't quite play out like it should have, well . . . welcome to entrepreneurship.

Some ideas to get you back on track:

1. **Adapt via frequent course corrections.** Having frequent "course correction" meetings allows you to check on plans and adapt them. Respond quickly to unexpected shifts like unforeseen events, bad assumptions, changes in the market, shifting customer buying patterns, cash flow issues, or new competitive threats.
2. **Adapt by challenging your assumptions.**
   - Get an advisory board.
   - Join a CEO group.
   - Find a trusted adviser like a retired CEO.
3. **Adapt by observing industry changes.** Observe and monitor market forces such as:
   - Sales trends
   - Consumer spending habits
   - Competitors' major product releases
   - Supplier issues

    - Talent management
4. **Adapt by instituting a reconnaissance function** that provides more data to test your assumptions. Ideas could include:
    - Joining your industry association and keeping track of trends, challenges, and issues.
    - Having your salesforce present quarterly recon debriefings.
    - Buying stock in a competitor's company if it's public. You only need one share to get access to stockholder data.
    - Investing in an online competitive database service.
    - Flattering a competitor and asking how they did it. Usually, they'll tell you!
5. **Adapt quickly by implementing quarterly progress meetings** to see what's working and, more importantly, what's not.
    - Check the status of your top strategic priorities or key performance indicators (KPIs).
    - Identify what's on course? Off course?
    - For what's off course: Why? What did you learn?
    - Identify the necessary course corrections.
6. **Adapt by having "lose powerfully" moments after every mistake or upset to the plan.** From my tour with the Pentagon and work with Matt Eversmann, I became impressed with what they call an after-action review (AAR). They used an AAR after every military encounter to learn from what went right and what didn't.

To help you create your own list of AAR questions to use after every situation, here's a starter set:

- What could we have done differently?
- What new information did we gain?
- Which assumptions did we make that weren't accurate?
- What did we think was real when it was just an illusion?
- How could we have tested our assumptions and realities better?
- Could we have recognized the warning signals earlier? And why did we ignore the warning signals?
- What will we do differently next time?

Case Study: Interview with Seth Greene

It's risky to adapt a plan. Just ask entrepreneur Seth Greene. He took a risk—not only to change course but to do so against his wife's advice (now *that's* a risk-multiplier!). After graduating from college, Seth began working for a Fortune 500 financial services company. On his first day in the office after completing his training, his branch manager welcomed him to the firm by handing him a fat phone book and saying, "They're all in there, tiger. Go get 'em!"

Seth was on fire. He made three hundred cold calls every day for years, interrupting strangers, asking them for money. The result of his hard work?

Failure.

Seth was ranked 6,700th in the firm when it came to opening new accounts. Not 67th—6,700th. He was miserable.

Seth's plan had been sound. Great Fortune 500 training and support. Why not stay the course? It had to get better someday. I mean, where else could he go but up?

But Seth didn't stay the course.

He adapted.

Seth met up with legendary marketing guru Dan Kennedy.

Afterward, he went home and told his wife, "Honey, I know we just got married a year ago, and nine months ago we bought our first house, and three months ago we had our first baby, and three weeks ago you quit your job to be a stay-at-home mom, and I'm the sole breadwinner . . . but I want to borrow a whole bunch of money right now to hire this guy Dan, because I believe it will change our lives."

What was his wife's response? "For some strange reason she said 'no,'" Seth recalled with a chuckle. "I asked her the same question every day for thirty days in a row and her *no* kept getting more and more vehement, with other words inserted in between. But I am very persistent, and finally on day thirty-one she caved and said, 'You'd better pray this works.'"

So on a wing and a prayer, Seth adapted his plan. He borrowed that "whole bunch of money" and worked closely with Kennedy, learning how to effectively market his financial services.

How did it work out? Within two years he went from being the 6,700th-ranked adviser at his Fortune 500 firm to being in the top 30 *nationwide*, making more than enough money to pay back the loan. He was featured in several industry trade journals, books, and magazines, and his phone started ringing off the hook with financial advisers calling to ask for tips on how to do what he was doing.

Today, Seth is the founder of Market Domination,[6] one of the fastest-growing marketing firms in the country. He's appeared on major television networks, been profiled in leading newspapers nationwide, and is the author of five bestselling books, including his latest, *Market Domination for Podcasting.* Seth's been nominated for marketer of the year in his industry three years running.

He could have just kept going with the original plan, but true entrepreneurs know you have to adapt in order to win.

Case Study: Shaahin Cheyene

A great example of how planning isn't everything is Shaahin Cheyene, otherwise known as the "Willy Wonka of Generation X." (As it happens, Shaahin's story is also a great example of how to move past the valley of the shadow of demotivation.) Shaahin's an inventor, documentary filmmaker, writer, and the founder of Accelerated Intelligence Inc., a company that develops brain health supplements. Want an example of how to capitalize on great schooling, family money, good connections, a safety net, and a terrific support network? Well, don't look here. Here you have a real entrepreneur and a great example of what happens when you find power in hopelessness.

Shaahin and his family emigrated from Iran in 1980 when he was five years old. A high school dropout, Shaahin eventually left home on a mission to figure out what he wanted to do with his life—probably something that most of us did at one point or another. But this was after his fifteenth birthday. He took with him nothing more than a backpack of clothes, an old lime green 1966 Lincoln Continental, and a lot of hope. Since he had no money, Shaahin bounced around from sofa to sofa, sometimes sleeping in the car or on the beach. Eventually he found a mentor who helped him determine that what he really wanted to do was start up and run his own business someday.

But here's the thing about Shaahin: He didn't want to wait until he grew up to become a businessman. He wanted to do it *now*, at age fifteen. So there was only one burning question remaining: What kind of business would it be?

"I knew I wanted to develop a product. I didn't know what kind of product at first," Shaahin says. "So I researched and I thought about it, and I decided I was going to make a pill—a smart pill—and it was going to be the greatest thing ever because I was going to put Albert Einstein's picture on it, and it was going to be awesome because there would be nothing else like it."

Shaahin developed the perfect plan. He knew it would work. He mapped out the whole path ahead. What could go wrong? There was just one minor problem. He knew he couldn't put Einstein's picture on his product without permission, so he located the Beverly Hills law firm in charge of the great physicist's estate and called to make an appointment. Using his best adult businessman voice, Shaahin told the receptionist that he was with so-and-so company and he was interested in licensing the Einstein image for use on a product he and his team were developing. The assistant gave him an appointment with one of the attorneys.

"I went out and borrowed a suit from one of the few friends I had at the time," Shaahin says. "It was old and way too big for me, but it was better than the clothes I had. I didn't have enough money to pay for the valet parking at the office building on the day of the meeting, so I had to park far away and take a bus. I got to this humongous building and went up to the law firm's suite and a nice receptionist in very expensive high heels offered me an espresso while I waited for my appointment. I had no idea what an espresso was, so of course I said, 'Yes, please.'"

After an hour and thirty minutes, the attorney finally poked his head out the office door and barked at Shaahin to come in. The first thing he said to the young man in the ill-fitting suit was "Where's your dad?"

"What do you mean?" Shaahin asked.

"Well, I thought this was a meeting for a supplement corporation. Who's the representative for the corporation?"

"That's me."

"What? How old are you?"

"I'm fifteen."

The attorney, a chubby, balding guy in his fifties, closed the door to his office, turned to Shaahin, and asked, "You don't really have a company, do you?"

"Yeah, I have a company."

"Are you incorporated?"

"Not yet, but I will be . . ."

"Do you have funding? Do you have a trademark or a patent? Do you have people behind you? Do you have an office, a manufacturer?"

The attorney proceeded to go through the very long list of all the things Shaahin didn't have, every step of the way crushing his plans, his hopes, and his aspirations. Shaahin hung in there, though. He stayed and listened. He had pretty thick skin; after all, he was a fifteen-year-old kid with the courage to leave home, sleep on beaches, and live out of a knapsack. Not much fazed Shaahin, but this lawyer was close to making him cry.

The attorney went on to tell Shaahin that without a college degree and work experience, it would be impossible for him to run his own company. *Impossible!* He told the teen to go home to his parents, get an education, and work at a job for a few years before trying to start a business.

"Once you've done all that, come see me and we can talk," he said. "But until then, no way." Then he patted Shaahin on the back and showed him the door.

Shaahin was crushed. With a failed plan, utterly dejected, without any hope on the horizon for his fledgling business, he walked back to his car. But a voice in his head kept telling him, *That guy's a jackass, but he's right. He's totally right. I don't have any of the stuff you need to start a company. What was I thinking? I just made a total fool of myself.*

Welcome to entrepreneurial hopelessness. No plan. No motivation.

Remember that "moment" I mentioned earlier? When you're facedown tasting the dirt?

That's the moment. The special moment. And what happened next is the magic of entrepreneurship. By the time

Shaahin reached his broken-down old car, another voice came into his head, and this one said, *You know what? Fuck that guy. He doesn't know anything. I'm gonna do it anyway. This is not how my life is gonna turn out. His reality doesn't have to be my reality. I am not giving up.*

"Everything the attorney said was true," Shaahin recalls, "but what he didn't understand was that I had nothing to lose. This lawyer had a Porsche Carrera and a fancy house in Malibu and all those expensive things that life has to offer, but I had nothing. I remember looking at my little backpack filled with old clothes and realizing that I could never get any lower than I was right then. And I was willing to suffer and sacrifice to keep going."

Shaahin is now super grateful to that pessimistic attorney, because he eventually took his product, Herbal Ecstasy, to market. And it was about time. Shaahin had reached the ripe old age of sixteen. Six months after that fateful meeting, and practically overnight, Shaahin was sitting on a company worth millions of dollars. A year later he was on the path to making hundreds of millions. A year after that he was running one of the largest supplement companies of its day—with two hundred employees and offices in thirty-two countries—and with revenues of well over $350 million a year.

Did it take decades to make it happen? No. Shaahin spent his eighteenth year on this planet doing talk show interviews with people like Sam Donaldson and Montel Williams. He appeared on the cover of *Newsweek* and was featured in a twelve-page spread in *People* magazine. As Shaahin Cheyene discovered, sometimes the destruction of a plan, and a little hopelessness, is all it takes to push you to the next level as an entrepreneur.

Seth and Shaahin discovered how to adapt, but they also found out, like many entrepreneurs, that you can *never stop* adapting your plan, even after you create a successful company.

DEBUNKED MANAGEMENT MYTH #3: PERSEVERE

When entrepreneurs are faced with demoralizing challenges and failed expectations, experts recommend they keep an optimistic attitude, use affirmations, practice positive thinking, reflect on motivational quotes, and any number of other methods to help you persevere.

But this all took a turn for me when, during a workshop, one CEO asked a funny question: "Why is perseverance a virtue? Why can't 'giving up' be a virtue?"

Sardonic, but something about it got my attention.

All success stories show how entrepreneurs persevered, but when I did autopsies on dead companies, something emerged that I'd never seen published:

**A lot of dead companies persevered . . .
but far too long.**

Perseverance doesn't work all the time. Many dead companies persevered and stuck to their plans long after they should have given up.

But why didn't they give up?

Perception.

**Keeping old perceptions alive causes
death by perseverance.**

Persevere if you want, but if you're unable to perceive situations differently, stupid things happen. You keep thinking you're right, believing your way is the best, or thinking you know everything. Fix this problem or you're on your way to becoming an idiot.

Demystify

Resisting change in your perception stops you from seeing a day when your product or service will be irrelevant, or when another sales channel will outrun you (Amazon, anyone?). But why do entrepreneurs resist change?

Because of our biology. Two areas have been identified as the culprits.

The first is the hippocampus region of the brain. The early research on this began decades ago when Lou Tice began coaching executives on it. The hippocampus interacts with other brain regions, such as the neocortex, to determine which pieces of information are important and should be stored in long-term memory and which to ignore. This allows us to be more focused by filtering out less relevant information and keeping only more significant experiences and knowledge.

So what's the problem? When this part of our brains only focuses in one direction, it blocks out everything else, causing us to fail seeing threats or obstacles coming at us from other directions.

The second area of your biology that causes change resistance is the ego. Not a new idea. We've seen arrogant companies fall from greatness for years because they thought they were powerful and knew everything, and that their way was the right way.

But what can *you* do to prevent that? Time to become samurai.

I know this sounds crazy, but you're too far into this book to turn back now. My interest in the samurai emerged accidentally after returning from a Himalayan expedition. I stumbled onto an ancient manuscript that captured over seven hundred years of leadership training by the samurai. Oxford gave me permission to publish a book based on it, *The Code of the Executive.* It unexpectedly became a bestseller and was

translated into a dozen languages. The next thing I knew I was on CNN, MSNBC, and dozens of other news media channels. Go figure. MIT geek becomes literary celebrity.

Samurai warriors were among the fiercest in history, and new archaeological battlefield DNA evidence indicates that about one-third were women. They repelled Mongol invasions, lived by heroic codes of honor, had indifference to pain, and showed unflinching loyalty. Far more than just warriors, they were also extremely well-educated, highly literate, and skilled in mathematics and the arts. They knew how to overcome the ego. You've seen the samurai in movies like *The Last Samurai* with Tom Cruise or observed characters based on them in movies and shows like *Star Wars, Star Trek, Transformers, The Mandalorian,* and *Power Rangers.*

I was so grateful for the opportunity to unearth such long-buried wisdom—except for one problem. The first chapter was on . . . death. Showing CEOs and their teams how they can outperform competitive threats is one thing, but teaching them how to die properly? I hesitated.

But then I stopped resisting change to my perception.

After searching through many sources, I was unable to find any management theory to help me understand this. One professor at Hopkins said, "Maybe you just unearthed one of the most epic lost secrets to superior leadership ever discovered."

"This would mean introducing a concept contrary to current leadership thinking," I said. "I wouldn't be very popular."

"When has disrupting the status quo ever stopped you?" he said.

He had a point. I couldn't ignore the evidence. In combining brain science with genetics and evolutionary psychology, I discovered how the concept of death unhooks our ego and allow us to change our perception. It isn't about the suicide rituals samurai were known for, but about committing suicide to the ego—what they called the evil spirit.

The ego unhooks when the need for its selfish genetic strategy for committing genetic warfare (DNA replication) ends. And that comes at physical death. The samurai method was really not performing ritual suicide (yet) but to achieve the same ego release by simply remembering to "keep in mind constantly, day and night, that someday you must die."

I know. Not a typical management training concept, but after teaching this to thirty thousand CEOs, it still hits the mark. Applying this in corporations produces increased speed of strategic execution, decisiveness, and perception change by over 300 percent.

How? By eliminating those selfish attachments of the ego that drive politics, power, fear, domination, being right, looking good, blaming, avoiding accountability, and all those dysfunctions that suck velocity and focus out of our companies. When remembering death unhooks those attachments, we achieve what's been missing in leadership development: Bravery, honor, and speed.

In leadership, death is not to be feared.
It is freedom.

The greatest armies, leaders, and executive teams know that death before battle makes you dangerous to the enemy and unleashes personal growth. Steve Jobs summed it up well:

> Remembering that I'll be dead soon is the most important tool I've ever encountered to help me make the big choices in life.
>
> Almost everything—all external expectations, all pride, all fear of embarrassment or failure—these things just fall away in the face of death, leaving only what is truly important.
>
> Remembering that you are going to die is

> the best way I know to avoid the trap of thinking you have something to lose. You are already naked. There is no reason not to follow your heart.
>
> No one wants to die. Even people who want to go to heaven don't want to die to get there. And yet, death is the destination we all share. No one has ever escaped it, and that is how it should be, because death is very likely the single best invention of life. It's life's change agent. It clears out the old to make way for the new.

So unhooking your hippocampus and ego allows you to shift your perspective and not keep perseverance alive past its expiration date.

Persevere, yes, until it's time to accept death.

How to Lose Powerfully Now That You Know That Perseverance Isn't the Only Option

Persevering makes sense when it works, but stubbornly holding on when you should be letting go stops you from losing powerfully because:

- You'll fail to adapt.
- You'll never achieve any learning.
- No amount of additional suffering will save you.

How can you investigate whether you should stop persevering?

Simple:

1. Always keep an open mind to market and competitive changes, even in areas not part of your current focus.
2. Study and meditate on those philosophies that shed light on the power of detachment. Beyond samurai, such insights exist in studies of Buddhism, Stoicism, Christianity, Taoism, Sufism, Advaita Vedanta, humanism, Hinduism, Epicureanism, and mindfulness.
3. Do a head-check on your thoughts. Do you:
   - Think you're right? (If so, how do you validate that?)
   - Believe your way is the best? (Have you pilot-tested your idea yet?)
   - Think you already know everything? (This one is most dangerous. Stop it.)
4. Discern between smart perseverance and idiotic stubbornness. Here's your checklist:
   - Have you expended far too much time and money?
   - Has the effort produced no new insights?
   - Has progress stopped or never been observed in the first place?
   - Are you no longer having fun?
   - Are you learning or just feeling frustrated?
   - Are you growing or feeling stifled?
5. Identify specifically what you should be letting go of.
   - What projects or goals have outlived their usefulness?

- Where are you wasting time trying to get things to work long after they should have died?
- Which partners have you held onto far too long?
- Who are the people who might have helped you get here but won't get you there?
- What vendors are you holding onto that never brought the value you had hoped—or they did but now seem to be a burden?
- Which customers are more of a distraction to growth than part of it?

Ask yourself what in your life must die so you can move to the next level.

Like the old samurai saying in my book *The Code of the Executive*, "When you leave your gate, act as though an enemy is in sight."

Case Study: Will Henshall

Will Henshall had a rude awakening that made it clear to him he needed to stop persevering and let an idea die. Interviewing him was a delight. "I had to be an entrepreneur. I'm the worst employee in the world!" he says. "I'm a five-times entrepreneur with the crazy profile of being a right-brain musician and left-brain scientist." Being accused of some of this myself, I immediately hit it off with him.

A successful musician and composer,[7] Will was born in the UK, the latest in a long line of entrepreneurs—seven generations, in fact. His ancestors spearheaded a whole range of lucrative ventures, from steam engines to radios to TV. Entrepreneurialism was in his DNA.

"I was online in the eighties before anyone else. I started Rocket Network in 1994 and created the collaborative network

of recording studios Digidesign. Paul Allen, Microsoft's cofounder, got involved with me, and it was so successful it ended up being integrated into the Avid worldwide music production equipment ProTools."

With a successful track record in software and engineering, Will decided to embark on another brave idea. He told me that he'd "never talked to any other writer about this before" and shared with me the most insane thing that had ever happened to him. It became a great example of the power of rejecting perseverance, and I was honored he would reveal this to me for this book.

"We noticed a lot of people reading on Kindle while listening to music. So I thought, why not create a soundtrack for a novel?" Will says. "You know, while readers are reading on the Kindle, instead of listening to random music, we play scary music during the scary parts, exciting music during exciting parts, sad music during . . . well, you get the idea."

Will started the "music for reading" venture, and it seemed destined for success. He raised $2 million in funding, got the attention of the CEO of Random House, and became involved directly with the Amazon Kindle team.

"Everyone thought it was the greatest idea; open up any book, hit the button, and get the right music for the right page as you read. I hired the former Avid/Digidesign CTO, brought on an amazing engineering team, and went to Amazon headquarters," Will says. "Amazon was amazed at how we'd hacked the Kindle and added a music button to their interface. We were ready to negotiate an annual seven-figure licensing deal."

Will Henshall was in the zone! The entrepreneurial dream solidly in front of him with great funding, the best engineering team in the world, a unique idea Amazon was very excited about and supported by stellar market and pricing research. Everything pointed to it being a slam dunk; the idea was a no-brainer.

What could go wrong?

People didn't want to pay for it.

"Worse. They didn't want it at all. About 10 percent said it was amazing, 10 percent said 'meh,' but 80 percent thought it was the stupidest fucking thing they'd ever seen! They said, 'This thing stops me from reading, and it's distracting and irritating!'"

"Wow. What did you do?" I ask.

"Well, I was stunned! I wondered how I could have missed this. It was a total failure."

Apparently, when reading a book, even though the music changes cleverly followed one's reading speed, the emotional content of the exciting soundtrack actually distracted people. Your brain responds to sound differently when you're reading than when you're watching a movie!

At this point, Will could have persevered. He could have done more market research, tried to tweak the music, fixed the product, resold the concept to Amazon, and doggedly pursued the idea. But instead, he let it die.

Letting go of perseverance can be scary. But sometimes you need to do it to move on. For Will, when he stopped persevering and let it die, something interesting happened.

Will said, "When you stopped reading, the system didn't know where you were in the story and it just played neutral music until you started reading again. People started calling me and telling me they left the music on in the background as they were working and it really helped them work better. People began writing to me to find out how they could just use this music at work."

With enough neutral music soundtracks, and a new idea for applying music scientifically as a productivity tool, Will went to Singularity University, founded by Ray Kurzweil,[8] Google, Cisco, and others (check them out at www.su.org). Not a bad place to bounce an idea around.

"Well, what happened?" I asked.

Will had his big aha moment.

"They were psyched! People get paid to work, not to read, and so we began developing the first version of 'focus@will.' We created more neutral music. But we went even further. We engaged neuroscientists and investors and became an SU Labs Accelerator company."

Today focusatwill.com offers a remarkable music system scientifically proven and designed to create specific audio streams to help people focus and concentrate, even people with ADHD. In fact, I've been using Will's music to write this book!

Case Study: Kim Song-il

Few entrepreneurs persevere with their first idea and get lucky. Most of the successful ones have given up on that initial idea and gone on to create something newer and better.

The life of Kim Song-il, an entrepreneur now onto his seventh business, is the perfect example of how stopping persevering and giving up can save your life. Kim defected from North Korea fourteen years ago. He had a plan, but it didn't quite work out. South Korean soap operas sold a dream, but the real world was very different. Where was the glamorous life? Where was the better world he'd been expecting?

He couldn't exactly go back to the misery, or possible imprisonment or death, in North Korea. I understood Kim Song-il's situation. I saw North Korea across the DMZ (demilitarized zone), and even reached the two-kilometer mark of the DMZ in an underground tunnel with my kids. I take my children around the world on various research trips, promising that they'll appreciate it when they're older (we'll have to wait and see how that works out). I want them to see the real world, to learn about other societies and forms of government by seeing

them with their own eyes, not through the lens of US bias. What made this trip more poignant was that my father had been a Korean prisoner of war. He crossed one of the bridges we saw from North Korea. I couldn't stop crying in front of that bridge.

The difference between North and South Korea couldn't be more dramatic. When Kim escaped the North and tried integrating into South Korean culture, he ran into an unexpected cultural clash that he found incredibly challenging. Being a former military officer in the North, Kim was used to giving orders. But giving and taking orders as an employee in a capitalist society is a very different experience to giving and taking orders in the North Korean military.

Having to work for everything instead of having it provided to you by the state often comes as a shock to escapees like Kim. What's the result of North Korean defectors dealing with these challenges in the South?

High suicide rates.

Kim Song-il could've followed that path, but he:

- First tried to survive by becoming a bus driver
- Gave up on pursuing that goal and became a laborer
- Gave up on that and ran a restaurant
- Gave up on that and now he's running his own business selling chicken pieces. He buys whole chickens and has a handful of employees cut them up and bag them for freezing. This product is then sold, the price of the parts combined being greater than the cost of the whole.

Was it easy for Kim? No. A lot of suffering and sacrifice. He eventually even reconsidered his suicide. After the failure

of his earlier businesses, he attempted suicide three times. But he hung on to the fact that he had risked everything to get to South Korea.[9]

Constantly adapting his plans and knowing when to stop persevering enabled him to survive the struggle. Kim's experience shows us what real entrepreneurship requires.

Case Study: Me

Many times I held on too long, keeping projects alive that should've died long ago. But when I let go, life changed. One example gave birth to my book *The Code of the Executive*. Over twenty-five years ago I was working on another book focused on tribal leadership. Frustrated from a back-and-forth debate with my agent on the manuscript, I left the US for that expedition in the Himalayas I mentioned earlier. I wanted to find out if this once-lost civilization, Bhutan, managed their organizations similar to how we do—an indicator of biological leadership patterns.

While trekking in the most remote mountainous regions—sleeping on the ground, living in tents, and not seeing electricity or a toilet for a month—our team spent the nights resting while the sherpas prepared a meal of yak meat and red rice. Out of boredom one night, we played a Tibetan fortune-telling game where we had to present a life problem. When it was my turn I chose my frustration with my agent, threw the pieces of wood, and the game came back with an answer: Give up so you can move on.

Give up? Stop persevering?

Initially stunned at the response, I couldn't ignore the answer. The Tibetan gods had spoken! I didn't want to piss off the gods (I already had enough problems), so I returned to the United States, called my agent, and buried the project.

What happened after I stopped persevering? A few weeks

later I discovered an ancient samurai manuscript and contacted Oxford University, which graciously gave me copyright permission, and I published *The Code of the Executive.* If I had persevered with the tribal leadership book project, I probably would've given up writing, and you wouldn't be holding this book in your hands now.

True perseverance is great, but it's also great to accept a lot of deaths when the time comes.

Don't let holding on hold you back from winning.

DEBUNKED MANAGEMENT MYTH #4: HAPPY EMPLOYEES

John bounded off stage after his gripping speech at the company's annual conference. As CEO, he was proud that their new employee initiative had finally been launched. His team had spent so much time and money on culture-change consultants that they couldn't wait to see the results of their new "happy-employee program." Like the experts say, if you keep employees happy, they'll keep customers happy.

Sure, doing things like providing competitive compensation, encouragement to grow, a positive work environment, recognition, and appreciation builds employee self-esteem and makes them comfortable—a good foundation for success. But John felt surprisingly uneasy as he walked back to his table.

Sitting down, he maintained a smile as the vice president of HR got up on stage next to lay out the program details. As he pretended to be paying attention, his brain wrestled with a troubling thought: *We're so focused on happy employees, have we ignored the fact that the world's not perfect?* He knew

that market challenges and new competitors were emerging. Things were going to get tough. *Did we forget to ask a dangerous question?* He grabbed a napkin and a pen:

What will our employees do when they're not happy?

No motivational speaker ever posed *that* question! But that's *the* question!

John's fear represents what one entrepreneur said over dinner after my keynote, "If the going gets tough and my happy employees aren't happy anymore, will they join me in the fight or turn and run, leaving me on the field alone?"

Good question. But isn't it your job to make sure employees are comfortable? Aren't you supposed to suffer alone to protect them from the mistakes and failures that might make them unhappy? Doesn't winning require keeping your employees' self-esteem high?

Well, no. That's bullshit.

Demystify

To win, your employees need to know how to lose powerfully, even if it makes them unhappy. Otherwise, when they get demotivated by failure, you get sucked into doing their job, and then emotion—not strategy—rules the day.

Winning should never be separated from losing. You need both, and they are burned into the lives of every great entrepreneur. Protecting your people from losing in order to keep them comfortable and positive and build their self-esteem always ends badly.

What's the best proof of this? Let's look at a recent social experiment. A few thought leaders had the bright idea that

protecting kids from experiencing losing would boost their self-esteem. They believed that rewarding activity rather than results would improve society. The pivotal event was in 1986 when California legislator John Vasconcellos (Vasco) steered a bill to establish the California Task Force to Promote Self-Esteem and Personal and Social Responsibility, or the "Self-Esteem Commission." Vasco convinced people that low self-esteem was the cause of unemployment, educational failure, child abuse, domestic violence, homelessness, and gang warfare. He said that raising a population's self-esteem would be a "social vaccine," saving the state billions.

The movement spread.

By the end of the eighties, a large proportion of the US and UK abolished the idea of losing (failing, making mistakes, dealing with right versus wrong). Parents and educators set off on a mission to save the world. Everybody received an equal prize for their efforts, not their results, so that, in effect, everyone won. Kids grew up being told by their parents and teachers how wonderful and special they were. To get them to believe they were intelligent, important, talented, beautiful, and inherently good, changes were implemented in schools like:

- School awards being based on participation, not results.
- Ds and Fs being replaced with participation awards.
- Red pens being forbidden. They were far too "aggressive."
- Competitive sports being eliminated because kids couldn't cope with the pressure to win.

This is not a *Saturday Night Live* skit or an *Onion* headline. This really happened.

Vasco's plan backfired spectacularly.

A growing body of research now finds that the self-esteem movement didn't help kids. It hurt them:

- In the US, the first-year *A* average in high schools rose from 18 percent to 48 percent as SAT scores fell.[10]
- Keith Campbell, professor of psychology at the University of Georgia,[11] found that building up self-esteem while neglecting to support attainment does not serve our youngsters well. He said, "We live in a world of trophies for everyone. Fourteenth-place ribbon. My daughter got one."[12]
- Narcissism rose, as evidenced by selfie-snapping millennials.
- Gifted students severely underestimated their own abilities, adopted lower standards for success, expected less of themselves, underrated the importance of effort, and overestimated how much help they needed from a parent.
- Esteem-building praise of failing college students caused their grades to sink even further.
- Giving kids the label of "smart" did not prevent them from underperforming. In fact, kids who were told they were "smart" ended up performing less well in tests than before after they'd been given this label.
- Scholars from Reed College and Stanford University found that praised students become reluctant to take risks and don't think that they have much autonomy. They are also less persistent, exhibit more "eye-checking with the teacher," and inflect their words so that "answers have the intonation of questions."[13]
- Research from esteemed psychologist and author

> of international bestseller *Mindset* Carol Dweck found that for overpraised kids,[14] image maintenance becomes their primary concern, and they are more interested in tearing others down.

Reviews of two hundred studies of children being protected from losing in order to boost their self-esteem concluded that their grades and career achievement didn't improve, and it did not lower violence of any sort.

One particular school in Lancashire, England—Barrowford Primary—found themselves the target of mockery for their rigorous adherence to, and the subsequent spectacular failure of, their own self-esteem program when, in 2014, they wrote to pupils who didn't perform so well in their exams:

> These tests do not always assess all of what it is that make each of you special and unique. . . . They do not know that your friends count on you to be there for them or that your laughter can brighten the dreariest day. They do not know that you write poetry or songs, play . . . sports, wonder about the future, or that sometimes you take care of your little brother or sister after school.[15]

Teachers were discouraged from punishing or defining a child as "naughty" or raising their voices. The kids were to be treated with "unconditional positive regard."

But that wasn't enough. On their sports day, all the year groups were handed participation ribbons. WTF is a participation ribbon?

Did all the good intentions and nurturing of self-esteem translate into higher achievement?

No.

The result: An assessment report found that the school had "emphasized developing pupils' emotional and social well-being more than the attainment of high standards." In 2015, the school received the lowest teaching ratings and the lowest exam results.[16]

All this self-esteem mess ends up spilling over into simple events like children's parties. Australia's *Child* magazine[17] published an article in which the friend of a mother who had the outrageous idea of only having *one* prize in a Pass the Parcel game at a party described the fallout.

> She said, "I'm so tired of this 'you're-all-winners' mentality . . . Kids need to learn that life isn't always fair."

When the game ended with only one child winning, each child used to the "everyone wins" approach became hysterical and couldn't be consoled. One girl stomped and screamed, "I don't like to lose. I never lose!"

This lack of correlation between self-esteem and social and academic skills eventually made researchers such as Nicholas Emler of the London School of Economics and Roy Baumeister of Case Western Reserve University reach what are now obvious conclusions. Their study found that schools and parents focusing on building self-esteem by protecting children from experiencing failure didn't result in higher achievement. On the contrary, high self-esteem may contribute to low academic scores.[18] Baumeister was quoted as saying his findings were "the biggest disappointment of my career."

Allow me to augment these scholarly publications with my own pub research. No, not publication research. Actual pubs. Hitting pubs in the countries I'm in provides great opportunities for "field research," and I do a lot of field research. What do I find? This lack of correlation between high self-esteem

and achievement exists everywhere. In one pub I made friends with some ex-cons who had lived in nice gated communities where you have to be indicted to be invited (the country's most notable prisons). What were their self-esteem levels? Surprisingly very high! A Florida State University study confirmed this too. They found criminals and drug abusers have higher self-esteem than the general population. Bullies even see themselves as superior to their classmates. Highly aggressive, violent people often think very highly of themselves, debunking the theory that low self-esteem can cause aggressive behavior.

What does my politically incorrect research conclude? The problem isn't that people lack self-esteem; they lack shame. The samurai research revealed that shame helps produce bravery. A coward with shame will go into battle because they don't want to be seen running away, and after a few battles they become brave.

What does this mean for you? Remember that it's not always about keeping everybody happy and building self-esteem. It's about everyone experiencing winning *and* losing; both essential experiences if we want children—and employees—to become real winners, successful entrepreneurs, high performers, and great people.

Biologically, it makes sense. As a species, we're meant to experience both winning and losing. It's what genetic warfare is all about.

Losing powerfully strengthens us as a species, and our civilizations emerge stronger for it.

How to Lose Powerfully Now That You Know It's not About Happy Employees

"Life is struggle."

—Karl Marx

Engage Your Employees in the Struggle

Stop saving your employees. Protecting them from failure:

- Weakens them
- Keeps them low
- Doesn't inspire them to rise to the challenge
- Dilutes the winners

Instead, engage them in the struggle and inspire them to take a risk by reaching for something greater. Feeling motivated is important, for sure. But when the going gets tough, help them embrace losing, learn from it, engage the suffering, feel the sacrifice, and show them how to pick themselves up again and keep moving.

That's what entrepreneurs do.

The point about struggle is no better demonstrated than in the work of *New York Times* bestselling author and entrepreneur Ben Horowitz. He was a former executive for companies like Loudcloud, AOL, and Netscape; board member on companies like Caffeine, Foursquare, Genius, Lyft, and Medium; and author of *The Hard Thing About Hard Things: Building a Business When There Are No Easy Answers.*

I think Ben knows what I'm talking about. He captured the entrepreneur's experience brilliantly in a piece titled "The Struggle":[19]

The Struggle is when you wonder why you started the company in the first place.

The Struggle is when people ask you why you don't quit and you don't know the answer.

The Struggle is when your employees think you are lying and you think they may be right.

The Struggle is when you don't believe you should be CEO of your company.

The Struggle is when you know that you are in over your head and you know that you cannot be replaced.

The Struggle is when everybody thinks you are an idiot, but nobody will fire you.

The Struggle is where self-doubt becomes self-hatred.

The Struggle is when you are having a conversation with someone and you can't hear a word that they are saying because all you can hear is The Struggle.

The Struggle is when you want the pain to stop.

The Struggle is unhappiness.

The Struggle is when you go on vacation to feel better and you feel worse.

The Struggle is when you are surrounded by people and you are all alone.

The Struggle has no mercy.

The Struggle is the land of broken promises and crushed dreams.

The Struggle is a cold sweat.

The Struggle is where your guts boil so much that you feel like you are going to spit blood.

The Struggle is not failure, but it causes failure. Especially if you are weak. Always if you are weak.

Every great entrepreneur goes through the Struggle. It's where greatness comes from, and it's the best way to lose powerfully.

Use Your Winning Saga

As we exposed the myth of the happy-employee movement and building self-esteem, we discovered something. You want to know what really makes employees happy?

Winning!

So, use your Winning Saga. When employees are engaged around a Winning Saga, they can lose powerfully and be willing to suffer and sacrifice with you. Great organizations don't win because their people are always happy. That's the easy stuff. They win because of their willingness to grind through it together for a greater strategic cause.

Look, I'm not saying all those motivational posters, T-shirts, and coffee mugs are useless. I'm not dismissing all those speakers who get standing ovations and leave their audiences excited to step up, step out, go for the gold, and win! I'm just saying that these things alone are not enough in the real world.

It's fun when your ship's docked in a safe harbor. But ships aren't built to stay in safe harbors.

It's what you do when you hit the shitstorm that matters. All that motivational stuff looks great until you're out of cash and out of time, banks are calling, scared employees are jumping ship, your company's driven into the rocks, and clients smell smoke. When your world starts crashing down like

that, all those podcasts, posters, and quotes no longer cut it. That's when you discover what you're made of. *That's* where the magic happens. Instead of worrying about that happy-employee thing, reach for your Winning Saga and remember that Japanese quote: "Fall down seven times, get up eight."

Create employee happiness from winning, not caretaking.

Prepare for Young Hires Who Always Expect to Win

What if you hire someone who's never experienced failure because they were raised during the failed self-esteem social experiment?

It could happen.

First, we don't want to paint all from the "self-esteem generation" with this brush (although stereotypes are a real time-saver). Many good parents didn't protect their kids, and those kids did learn a lot from losing and failure. Many raised their kids with discipline, consequences, boundaries, and the value of hard work.

But parents who fell under the "self-esteem spell" produced a generation that can become your future employees and customers. If so, you'll find people who are:

- Self-obsessed
- Unmotivated
- Lack work ethic out of a belief that it's not possible to lose and you should not have to work hard
- Feel they deserve the participation ribbons they've been handed as children
- Entitled
- Unprepared for the real world

I had a professor critique a PhD dissertation. Her student broke into tears. When asked what was wrong, the student said, "No one ever told me I did something wrong before."

Sadly, those who were raised to feel "special" must now deal with the reality that they aren't. If we take a more generous view, perhaps the self-esteem movement produced a disadvantaged generation:

Maybe these kids aren't entitled or lazy, but paralyzed by the fear of losing.

This has caused much conflict in the workplace. Work with HR to find ways to onboard and facilitate education, using the aforementioned research to coach employees who may experience losing for the first time while under your employment.

Keep YOU Ready for the Struggle

To keep yourself ready for battle so you're prepared to lead your people through the Struggle:

1. Meditate: The greatest warriors learn how to calm their mind for the battles ahead. Take time to be silent. There are a number of books and seminars on this. Choose one that works for you.
2. Body Health: You are useless if you cannot act on and lead your venture. Nothing new here you haven't heard before. Physical exercise and good nutrition. Get a trainer. Use your doctor. Schedule exercise on your calendar as you would a business meeting.
3. Drive your life using the Winning Saga you created. Remember it, meditate on it, pray from it. Let it drive your decisions.
4. Remember you're not alone.
    - Join a CEO group.
    - Involve your significant other or close friend to support you.

5. Help other entrepreneurs. Sharing the journey with another makes the path easier to walk.

Case Study: Marcus

One entrepreneur (we'll call him Marcus) knows about suffering and sacrifice. He set out to start a web-based sales management company. The market was ripe and opportunities were plentiful. He quit his job in the IT department of a large firm and rented out a cheap office in the suburbs. Using his savings and personal loans, he invested in the software, hardware, and offsite resources to make it all happen. At this stage, he was the epitome of positivity and motivation.

When I interviewed Marcus as part of my research, he said it was all going as planned "until the bank called me. That's kind of what happens when you stop paying on your loans. I wasn't surprised. I had several employees steal my intellectual property, which is what happens when you don't protect it with patents and trademarks. And then clients called because we missed a couple of critical milestones, and then my former employees went after my customers and clients too."

It wasn't a good time for Marcus. His dream was falling down a rathole.

"The bank was protected," he said. "I let them secure the loans with my house as collateral. . . . I had a delightful dinner conversation with my wife that night."

So, with all this going on, and more pain to come, Marcus quickly lost motivation. His life had collapsed.

At this point, many would have given up, gotten a job, found a bankruptcy attorney, and moved back in with Mom. But Marcus kept going. He put in over eighty hours a week to meet client demands, worked out advances with sympathetic customers to give him some runway to stay alive, sold his house, and moved into a small apartment.

"My family didn't see me for months. I slept at the office.

My life was work, food, sleep, work, food, sleep. I totally lost inspiration. I wasn't motivated. My joy turned to anger, fear, and desperation. I went back to my motivational podcasts and books, but they just didn't seem to help anymore. Instead, something deeper drove me," he said.

Marcus is not unusual. I hear this a *lot* from entrepreneurs who found themselves in a tough spot. And when I ask them what drove them, they don't describe it as motivation. It's something else.

Marcus kept going *in spite* of the anger, fear, and desperation. He suffered and sacrificed. He was not happy.

But he eventually made enough money to get restraining orders on former employees. Then he salvaged his clients, who, impressed with his willingness to sacrifice for them, sent him even more projects. He rebuilt his team, with appropriate safeguards on intellectual property and a better selection method based on their values. Eventually the suffering stopped and he regained positive motivation. He could grow his business out of passion, not fear.

He sold the business for a nice profit, and—a bit wiser—started another company soon thereafter.

Case Study: Doberman Dan's Tip for Using Routines to Keep a Saga Going

Doberman Dan came to entrepreneurship via an unusual route: law enforcement. As a police officer in Dayton, Ohio, back in the 1990s, Dan began toying with the idea of self-employment. He'd always been intrigued by the idea of being his own boss, and he'd also come to the realization that he didn't enjoy police work as much as he thought he would. So although he didn't know what the heck he was doing, he started a series of businesses out of his house.

All of them failed.

Dan had no choice but to keep plugging away at the police

department even though he disliked it. The only part of the job he enjoyed was writing crime reports. He was so good at it that his sergeant suggested he become a writer.

"He told me my arrest reports read like fiction," Dan says. "It was true. I absolutely loved writing those reports."

His sergeant's encouragement opened Dan's eyes to the possibility of writing for money. In 1997 he discovered direct response marketing (DRM) and copywriting and decided to give it a try. Since bodybuilding was a hobby of his at the time, his first creation was a self-published manual for bodybuilders, which he intended to promote using DRM.

"That manual was so bootstrapped," Dan says. "I printed the first copies on my little HP printer on three-hole paper. I even made my own cover. I stuck it all in a binder and sold it."

Lo and behold, the manual started making Dan some money. A year later it was generating enough to free him from his law enforcement job. The self-described "serial kitchen-table entrepreneur" has been starting and promoting successful businesses from his home ever since.

Dan discovered his personal Winning Saga to use his writing to help people sell. And he applied it to himself. He's started four nutritional supplement businesses, three of which he's sold; publishes the *Doberman Dan Letter* for direct response marketers and copywriters; produces a popular podcast for entrepreneurs called *Off the Chain*; and does DRM and copywriting for clients, including a $600 million-a-year company that recently hired him to help them start a new supplement division.

It takes a lot of energy and focus for Dan to keep all those balls in the air at once. It takes a lot of discipline to stay motivated. Over the last twenty years, Dan's come up with some interesting tricks for maintaining (or regaining) his motivation.

"I would love to tell you a sexy story about an instant magic-pill fix for getting the work done," Dan says. "I've looked

for the magic pill, but I haven't found it. Instead, my solution has been *my routine*. When I get out of my routine, everything falls apart. But when I stick to it no matter how I feel—which I admit is not easy to do—magic happens. I'd like to be 100 percent compliant on that, but some days life gets in the way. Still, if you're just 90 percent compliant, it's amazing what you can produce."

There are three important elements to Dan's daily routine. The first is based on a classic concept in financial planning.

"I have to balance my own business with the work I do for my clients, so I use the financial planning principle of 'pay yourself first,'" Dan explains. "When you get paid, you don't pay your bills first, you pay yourself 10 percent or whatever. I'm using that same principle with my time. I don't do any client work first thing in the morning. I always pay myself first by working on my own business, by sitting down and writing my newsletter as soon as I wake up."

The second part of Dan's daily routine has to do with the amount of time he devotes to each task, which is exactly thirty-three minutes and thirty-three seconds. He literally sets a timer and blocks out thirty-three-minute intervals on his calendar.

"I totally stole that thirty-three-minute/thirty-three-second thing from one of the most successful copywriters ever, Eugene Schwartz," Dan says. "He'd done a lot of study in advanced learning techniques and focus, and he said he found it really difficult to focus on things for more than a half hour at a time. So he set a timer for thirty-three minutes and thirty-three seconds, and I just swiped it. I figured, if it's good enough for that guy it's certainly good enough for me."

In essence, Dan makes appointments with himself. He blocks out the first thirty-three minutes and thirty-three seconds of his day for his newsletter, followed by a scheduled ten-minute break. Then it's another thirty-three minutes and

thirty-three seconds for the next task and another ten-minute break. He calls it a "mental psych-out," because no matter how unmotivated he's feeling, he knows he has to tolerate each task for only thirty-three minutes.

The final element of Dan's daily routine might be considered somewhat strange and even a little extreme, but he swears by it. It's something he learned during his old musclehead days as a bodybuilder. Dan doesn't eat anything past nine o'clock at night. When he wakes up in the morning, he drinks a glass of water and makes a four-cup pot of coffee. He puts the hot coffee in the blender with half a stick of butter (sometimes adding coconut oil too) and gives it a whirl, and then he drinks it. Seriously. No sugar, no cream. Butter. Dan doesn't ingest anything else until lunchtime; he just drinks the coffee with the butter.

"A guy named Dave Asprey came up with a name for this," Dan explains. "He calls it Bulletproof Coffee. You get the initial boost from the caffeine, and since you haven't eaten, a lot of people—myself included—find it gives a mental boost as well. It helps with focus and motivation. It's not just the surge from the caffeine, it's something about fasting for twelve hours or longer and then ingesting the combination of the caffeine and the fat from the butter. There are all kinds of hormonal things going on that I can't explain. All I know is that it works for me."

Pay yourself first, set a timer, make appointments with yourself, and drink Bulletproof Coffee—that's Doberman Dan's recipe for preventing the destruction of motivation, and also his recovery method for the inevitable times when motivation leaves you despite your best efforts.

"This routine is not easy to do at first," he says. "But if you can do it for just twenty-one to thirty days, you'll get in a groove and the sailing will become so much smoother. It's never easy, but it will be smoother. If you can discipline yourself to do it

every day for a month, it really does get easier after that."

I also found this out for myself when it came to my advisory group, Strategic Growth Alliance. We do a lot of strategic planning for companies, and they leave with a great road map. We warned them that it doesn't end there—that this is only the beginning. But eventually we learned that we needed quarterly sessions *after* the strategy retreat to ensure they were adapting the plan as reality hit.

You yourself will know how important it is to keep adapting if you've ever worked with a company that had a planning session and never revisited those minutes again or put any of the action points in motion.

Don't put too much energy into planning. Put more into adaptation. Remember Chris Warner, mentioned earlier? He launched one of the most successful climbing gyms in the country from a plan written on toilet paper while he was stuck in a tent on the side of a mountain during a storm.

All this adaptation is challenging, I know. It requires you to keep persevering. That's your next big adventure.

DEBUNKED MANAGEMENT MYTH #5: BE THE LEAD DOG

"You never lose until you actually give up."
—Mike Tyson

Hundreds of motivational speakers and authors "inspire" us to be the leader, be first, be out front, and be on top.

How many times have you heard clever comments like "If you're not the lead dog, the view never changes!"? It's a classic. You want to be the lead dog or you're always looking at

someone's ass. Don't ever be one of the poor sons of bitches running behind the lead dogs.

The only problem is none of these motivational speakers or consultants ever ran a dog team. Time to expose another myth.

Demystify

My kids grew up skiing in Steamboat Springs, Colorado. With a legendary history of creating top competitive skiers, Steamboat's Olympic-level instructors help even the most difficult students, like me, improve!

Every year at Steamboat I'd take a break with my kids to run dogsled teams. We prefer to use Grizzle-T Dog & Sled Works to train us to mush better. They train dogs for the Iditarod, so let's just assume they know a little about dogsledding. I got so addicted to the sport that I try to find a dogsled facility whenever I'm in the mountains during winter.

Here's what I learned: the only poor sons of bitches on a dogsled team are the lead dogs!

Why?

Dogs behind the lead dogs are doing everything but looking at the lead dog's ass! They're enjoying side views, pulling off to one side or the next, barking at each other, and totally ignoring the poor leaders in front trying to keep them on the trail. On one trip, a couple dogs jumped over the gangline (it attaches the dogs' harness tuglines to the sled) and again failed to follow the lead dogs. The team became imbalanced and pulled too hard running to the left, going off trail into deep snow and a ravine. This means a sled tip—but my five-year-old son was inside! It became scary real fast. I stood on the snow brake pad, but it failed to grip in the deep snow, and

we were getting deeper. My training kicked in and, to balance in this emergency, I quickly hopped on the runners on the opposite side, stood up, and leaned backwards, hanging on with my arms outstretched to counterbalance the weight and prevent flipping (kind of like burying the rail in sailboat racing). Realizing the crisis, a snowmobile zoomed past and halted the team. They rotated the dogs, who still refused to look at the lead dog's ass, but we now had a more controlled team.

At another training facility, we were one of the first dog-sled teams to have a head-on collision. Another team coming around the bend in the opposite direction met us straight on. Guess who the poor suckers were to take the brunt of *that* mistake? Yes, the lead dogs.

So, ignore any speaker who says you want to be the lead dog. They've never run a dog team and have no idea what they're talking about. The lead dog position sucks!

I got another clue when I took my two corgis to doggie daycare one day. As a single dad with full custody after a brutal divorce, I needed help some days with the dogs. During one session I asked the owner about the "lead dog" thing. She laughed. "Nobody wants to be the lead dog. It's a pain in the ass having all these dogs follow you around. They are constantly bothered and look annoyed all day. So they try to avoid it!"

But, in need of more data, I went to another group to expose this myth: thirty thousand CEOs. They agreed. Imagine always trying to get everybody to follow, having the buck stop on your desk, being the one feeling pain and panic, feeling guilty going home and dumping on the spouse at the end of a long day. Being the lead dog sucks!

So yes, we need lead dogs. And if you're one, you know it's a lot of work. But if you think the ones following you are going to follow your ass wherever it goes, you're in for a big surprise.

How to Lose Powerfully Now That We've Busted the Lead-Dog Myth

> "Jim-san. We all know you are a good manager, otherwise we would not have hired you. But please talk to us about your problems so we can all work on them together."
>
> —Fujio Cho, chairman of Toyota worldwide, when he ran the US Georgetown plant and had to "coach" a new American executive[20]

1. **Share your leadership.** That doesn't mean there won't be certain critical or emergency situations where you'll have to step in and direct, but most times you may be shouldering too much. In what areas can you delegate, outsource, start an ad-hoc team, or try other solutions to share the load?
2. **How much time are you spending getting sucked into operations?** Most of my audiences find they are sucked in way too much. We typically find when we work with companies that this pattern exists when the team under the leader is weak.
   - Is your team strong enough to delegate to?
   - If not, where are they weak?
   - What will it take to fix that? Training, coaching, restructuring? Or was someone promoted beyond their capacity to lead?
3. **Engage your people as soon as problems, mistakes, and other failures happen.** Let them help figure out the solution, learn, and spread the wisdom.

4. **How safe is it for them to bring their problems to you "so we can all work on them together"?** Sometimes problems fester too long because people are afraid to surface them. Developing a culture of openness and bravery fixes this.

DEBUNKED MANAGEMENT MYTH #6: HUMAN POTENTIAL

Believing in human potential is necessary for building great teams and organizations. Who can argue? It's in all the podcasts, webinars, and how-to books.

So what's the problem?

We need to ask, "The potential for what?" Potential can be good or bad.

We think somebody has potential to grow and fly, but how many times do they fail to lift off because they always run out of runway? What if they've already reached their highest level of potential? When people lack the capacity for higher potential, a longer runway never helps.

One CEO, Joyce, was compassionate. She hired George.

"I just started this company and needed to ramp up fast. George had a great résumé, passed the interview process with flying colors, and all the references checked out. But after six months, he clearly wasn't getting it," she said. "Projects got off course. Deadlines were missed. He talked a good game but couldn't get out of the bleachers and onto the field to run the ball with the rest of the team. It was shocking how he could screw the simplest things up."

And people started talking. "He's the result of a sperm that won?" "He's a disaster waiting to happen." "We don't have enough hazmat suits to protect the staff from him."

Joyce did what every concerned CEO does: made sure

George had a personal coach, read the top leadership books, watched TEDx Talks, participated in team-building exercises, and attended the best executive training programs. With no progress except George's extended vocabulary on the latest management lingo, Joyce had to accept that he had climbed higher than his capabilities were a fit for.

Joyce tried to move George to a lower-level position, but his ego couldn't handle it. He got another position in a company impressed with his extended vocabulary.

What happened? How come the best leadership development failed to develop George's human potential?

If you're like me, you've invested in a lot of books and seminars about developing the possibility of success in anyone. I really believed everyone had potential. I was all in. Nothing could stop me from seeking to build the potential of people and the possibility of extraordinary performance.

But one CEO—we'll call him Bob—found a problem with all this. He wanted to start a consulting practice. And he did. But it collapsed. Several times.

"My biggest mistake was believing people when they said they were great," he said. "I trusted them. And why not? They said they were terrific, had great résumés and wonderful stories about all the wonderful things they'd done. But in the end, they were my greatest self-inflicted wounds."

Believing that someone has potential just because they say so can be a problem. Bob just wanted someone to take over growing the consulting practice so he could spend more time researching, publishing, and speaking. In the end he lost over a million dollars on these people before he woke up. His failure list had grown too long:

1. Bob hired a husband/wife team from a top business school. The husband ran that business school's key global leadership initiative, and his

wife was top of her class. They knew a lot of F500 CEOs personally and even had a book out. These would be great partners for Bob. They certainly had potential! No-brainer, right? Wrong. They couldn't figure out how to grow sales or scale the programs. Their added costs ruined Bob's company in six months. I guess the only thing they forgot to teach in their business school was how to run a business.

2. A couple then joined Bob from the high-tech growth industry in Silicon Valley. One of them had successfully done a deal with Microsoft. So they sold Bob on the possibility of growing his business and the great potential they had for doing it. The last thing Bob remembers is them walking out after his net assets went negative.
3. A consulting company promised to monetize Bob's content and scale it. They'd have him online with a top branding platform and thousands of subscribers generating new sales by the end of the year. The problem was, after months of missed deadlines, Bob realized the consultants were over their head, and he was getting complaints about their quality of work from clients and staff. The consultants misrepresented what they were capable of, failed, and ran, dumping the project on Bob's secretary before it was complete. When Bob confronted them legally to get back the $50,000 he invested, they accused him of fraud because they said they didn't realize the resolution on his older films was too low, or didn't see all his content (even though they had all the passwords to all the content files and spent hours with Bob and his staff). That's like an agent representing

> a musician, failing, then suing the musician for fraud because the agent forgot to listen to the musician's songs first. For the first time in history a management consultant threatened to sue a client for fraud. Their reasoning was that the client was responsible for the consultants' failure to do due diligence before they took his money.

It was also bad with office staff. "More than once I had office staff with potential steal checks, lie about hours worked, take valuable assets, or fail to execute the most basic administration," Bob said. "They said they had potential but were masters at only one thing: excuses."

What did each person say to Bob after they devastated his company? Nothing. No apologies. No explanations for why they failed. Nada. They just kept the money he paid them and disappeared. And each time Bob had to sacrifice a year not doing valuable R&D so he could take over the business and turn it around . . . again and again and again.

Bob was a victim of believing in the potential of people. Everybody talks a good game when they're in the bleachers, but you don't know if they'll go facedown in the dirt until you put them on the field.

Why is this story important to me?

I'm Bob.

It was me.

I lost powerfully and learned a lot. Today I have a strong team and a new business model. But back then I was so consumed by research, publishing, teaching, speaking, and trusting others that I didn't have time to follow the proverb often quoted by Ronald Reagan:

"Trust, but verify."

Demystify

Everyone has potential, but only to their capacity. A lot of this is biological.

Dr. Elliott Jaques, psychoanalyst, social scientist, and management consultant, originated concepts such as corporate culture, midlife crisis, maturation curves, and time span of discretion organization. He studied medicine at Johns Hopkins University and social relations at Harvard University. Qualified as a psychoanalyst at the British Psychoanalytical Society, he was a founding fellow of the Royal College of Psychiatrists in Britain and visiting professor at George Washington University in Washington, DC.

I was introduced to Elliott's research by Dr. Jerry Harvey, professor of management science at the George Washington University. Eventually I was able to get Elliott to speak at my CEO group in Baltimore one day, but I never met him—had to get to New York for a CNN interview. Elliott's theory of cognitive complexity levels in the brain revealed why some people don't get it and have limited potential. Every human has a complex-thinking level measured by time span. Some people can lead a three-month project but fail with a one-year project. Others can lead a one-year project easily but not a three-year project. These levels of complex thinking show why people do not have unlimited potential, only the potential for the level of thinking they are on.

I'm oversimplifying deep psychological research, but this explained my failure in hiring. I assumed people knew what I was talking about when I hired them, but they bombed because they didn't have the complex thinking capacity level to understand what I said. They were great at week-to-week projects, but my five-year project was beyond their comprehension. This has nothing to do with intellect or skills. It's a totally different concept.

Another limitation to human potential is the person's willingness to do it. Not everybody is ready and may never be. Rick Jordan, another successful entrepreneur in the insurance industry and now with Unicity, said it best: "The biggest challenge is when you're working with the wrong people. We get so impressed, bring them on board, and put them in the business; we invest in them and then something happens. There's the *learning* curve but then there's the *doing* curve. Is this person willing to pay the price of personal improvement to get better? Do we tell them that they're not performing and if it doesn't get fixed, we're going to have a departure? You can tell who a winner is when they win. You want people who are willing to pay the price to get better."

How to Lose Powerfully Now That We've Busted the Human Potential Myth

Remember, you're not a state-funded "back-to-work" program to train the untrained. You can't afford it. Developing people's potential takes hundreds of hours. Great if you're a huge company, but you're not. You're an entrepreneur doing product development, marketing, sales, and a dozen other things. You think you have time to run a staff development program?

Also, even if someone wants to grow and develop their potential, you can't coach someone to be tall, and you can't fix stupid. So, when you make a hiring mistake, and you will, lose powerfully and learn from each one. It's a priceless education you can't buy anywhere else.

If you've already found this out too, don't worry. You're in good company. Whether they stole from you, failed to meet their grandiose promises, or just couldn't live up to their stated expectations of human potential, remember Hanlon's Razor:

"Never attribute to malice that which is adequately explained by stupidity."

Stop trusting what people tell you! We do a lot of trusting, but we don't sweat enough on verifying. *Everybody* gives a good story. Better to assume people don't know crap until they *show* it. Put them on the mat and see what they can do, and remember:

Let performance, not words, validate value.

In my speeches, the issue of hiring and retaining talent arises consistently. To ensure you avoid the human-potential myth and hire accurately, consider these tips:

1. **History Check:** When selecting a new hire, do a history check first. Interview those they worked with, but then ask them who else worked with the candidate (typically candidates only give you a sanitized list, so best to check with the people they did not mention). "Validating someone's history gives you insight into if they are coachable and can develop," Lou Tice said. "No one knows the limit of their own potential until they work to see how far they can go." Mark Panciera agrees, "Achieving potential is a lifelong passion, not always apparent on the surface, but a person's history tells the tale. What have they achieved? What's been their willingness to take chances or make an unorthodox decision? How have they developed their potential in the past? How did they handle success—or failure?"

2. **Behavioral Assessment:** A lot of online assessments are available that provide good snapshots of a person today. You can get insights into someone's personality type, behavioral tendencies, IQ, EQ, and projections of how people will respond in situations.
3. **Mindset Check:** Another area that limits human potential is the idea of "Mindset," a concept created by The Pacific Institute in the 1960s. To get deeper into how someone will behave in the future, Mindset matters. For example, a fixed Mindset is good when following rules is vital, like safety situations in the workplace, but if *too* fixed, it stifles vital creativity. How do you do a Mindset Check? One way is to just listen. Reactions are programmed into our subconscious by the way we think, so don't be afraid of asking tough questions. Tossing "softballs" won't get you much information for a hiring decision. Their reactions tell you what you need to know, so to identify traits and attitudes that reveal someone's Mindset, look for these things:
    - Do they ask questions about where the organization is headed?
    - Do they ask where you are heading?
    - Do they have any idea where they are heading?
    - How would they solve a particular problem or challenge you're presenting?
    - Are they aware of past mistakes and how they learned from them?
    - How far out in the future are they planning their life and career?

4. **Simulation Test:** Provide a case-study project for them to do and see how they perform.

Remember, bring people on board, but don't get too excited about their stories of great potential until you *see* what they can do. Pay them well for performance. Fire them fast otherwise.

NOW CREATE A WINNING WORLD

"Every great dream begins with a dreamer. Always remember, you have within you the strength, the patience, and the passion to reach for the stars to change the world."

—Harriet Tubman, nineteenth-century American abolitionist and social activist

Congratulations! Now you know how to win by using the power of losing and by busting the myths stopping you.

But it's not game-over yet. Time to recognize what significant impact entrepreneurs like you have on the world. I started discovering clues for this hidden effect accidentally (like most of my discoveries) during many of my crazy expeditions and excursions to remote regions of Africa, South America, Asia, and the Himalayas. I don't do these trips so I can post selfies, fill up passports, or collect T-shirts—although I do have a lot of T-shirts. Many of these journeys suck. The experiences are often uncomfortable, sometimes painful or extremely risky. Like when I almost got arrested as a capitalist spy in the Soviet Bloc, or got trapped during a riot in South Africa, or had my

camera fail while I was freezing at an altitude where the oxygen level dropped by 50 percent, or was chased by a bull elephant, or was jogging on a dirt runway in Africa trying to get back to camp before I started looking like "food," or stumbled onto a remote tribe and wondered how they were going to deal with me.

None of this is in the fancy travel brochures.

But why do I do these things?

To learn more about you. Our species.

While researching how cultures changed during the clash of Christian, Jewish, and Islamic shifts in Spain's history, I flew to the island of Mallorca. Because of its strategic location as a crossroads between Europe, Africa, and the Middle East, as well as its natural harbors, Mallorca was a significant launching point for long ocean voyages—a perfect area to research entrepreneurs.

During the Middle Ages and the Renaissance, many of the world's well-known explorers set sail from Mallorca. Some "customers" included Christopher Columbus, Ponce de Leon, and Hernando de Soto. So, if you got tired of Europe and wanted to discover unknown lands, it was probably a good idea to hang out in Mallorca and catch a ride.

While touring with a local academic I hired, we turned a corner and passed a small church. In front was a statue of a priest. It wasn't a big one, and I almost missed it.

"Who's this?" I asked the guide.

"That was one of our local priests," she said.

"Oh, was he the founder of this church?" I asked.

"Well, he founded a lot of missions. Some in your country," she said.

"Oh. Which ones? I travel a lot and visit many small towns. I might've come across one or two," I said.

"During the eighteenth century he founded a few, like San

Diego, San Antonio, Santa Clara, San Francisco. Have you visited them?" she said with a slight grin.

My jaw dropped.

Father Junípero Serra was an entrepreneur crazy enough to get on a boat from that island and risk sailing around the world to seek new lands. Would we have those great cities if he stayed in that humble church? If he feared loss? If he resisted change?

There were several other clues about the entrepreneurial impact on the world:

Clue: In the African Kalahari desert, they call October the "month of death." Water from the Angolan rains stops flowing into the region, the ground dries up, and animals face only two options: migrate or die. Even with such scarcity, one tribal community doesn't migrate. I visited a small village to see how they lived and organized for survival. As soon as I arrived they asked me an unexpected question: Did I want a Coke? What?

Clue: Among the tapestries in an Ecuadorian village, I suddenly noticed designs in some that weren't tribal but seemingly modern geometric repeating patterns. I asked where they'd gotten the idea. Apparently, a famous artist (Escher?) had trekked through there years earlier. His ideas spread, and their art forms evolved to incorporate his technique.

In Spain I saw Islamic mosaic patterns similar to the ones I'd encountered in North Africa. Inquiring further, I was told that wealthy rulers often exchanged talent and knowledge of their arts, so these shared patterns between continents were not unusual. This mutual sharing of information helped evolve their architecture and tools.

Clue: In a remote Himalayan village, families graciously

allowed us to enter their homes. I noticed their teenage daughter was doing homework. Leaning over, I asked her what she was studying in school. She said "Woodstock." WTF? They were learning about American culture, economics, trends, and music a world away.

Clue: In Vietnam several years ago, I felt an active entrepreneurial, capitalistic spirit the moment I hit Saigon. This wasn't the communism I was taught to fear as a child or what I had experienced in the Soviet Bloc in the eighties. Outside my hotel window was a Versace luxury retail store, and US fast-food franchises dotted the avenues. I saw a couple of first-release movies in 3D, met US CEOs who had moved their plants to Vietnam from China, and discovered that Vietnam's biggest trading partner was the US! Earlier, in May 2015, US Secretary of Defense Ash Carter and Vietnamese Defense Minister General Phùng Quang Thanh signed a joint vision statement on bilateral defense relations. They agreed to "expand defense trade between our two countries, potentially including cooperation in the production of new technologies and equipment." And I read soon thereafter that they had negotiated the placement of US Navy warships in Vietnamese harbors.

Even though my original research focused on how leadership occurred throughout human evolution, these clues opened up unexpected, and often inconvenient, insights. No matter which country, culture, or tribe I visit, I feel like there's a dragon always hiding beneath the ancient dust and artifacts. Its breath has the power to stop wars, reduce hunger, tackle ignorance, curtail disease, improve the quality of life, and ease poverty. It triggers beneficial exchanges of beliefs, ideas, skills, technologies, materials, art, tools, knowledge, cuisine, and culture between groups of humans.

It's the dragon of *trade,* also known by different names such as commerce, business, or mercantilism.

And who feeds this beast? It's not political or religious leaders.

It's you. The entrepreneur.

The evolution of civilization occurs when entrepreneurs risk creating new organizations, products, tools, and services, and they exchange their ideas with others. About twenty years ago this theme was eloquently captured by Jared Diamond, professor of geography and physiology at UCLA, in his Pulitzer Prize–winning book *Guns, Germs, and Steel.*

The power of business transforms civilizations.

What would the world look like if entrepreneurs didn't take risks, seek unfamiliar regions, or share new knowledge? Some set out to start a business, others set out to start an idea. Explorers of geography, engineering, arts, and sciences are entrepreneurs. Sakichi Toyoda, Columbus, Magellan, Soichiro Honda, Marco Polo, Buckminster Fuller, Jack Ma, Tesla, Steve Jobs, Einstein, Marie Curie, Oppenheimer, and Darwin are well-known, but history reveals many ancient entrepreneurs whose innovations and ambitions left a lasting impact on the world:

King Solomon (c. 970–931 BC): King of Israel who had building projects and a fleet of ships that traveled to distant lands for trade with other nations.

Cyrus the Great (c. 600–530 BC): Founder of the Achaemenid Empire, one of the largest empires in ancient history, he was known as an astute businessman who implemented economic reforms that helped to stimulate trade and commerce throughout his empire.

Zhang Qian (c. 200–114 BC): Chinese diplomat and explorer credited with opening up the Silk Road, a network of trade routes that connected China with the Mediterranean world.

Mithridates VI of Pontus (135–63 BC): King of Pontus, in the northeastern region of ancient Rome, expanded his kingdom through trade, including developing the region's silk trade with China.

Du Shi (c. ??–38 AD): Chinese polymath known for his contributions to hydraulic engineering, metallurgy, and the production of gunpowder, iron, and steel.

Cai Lun (c. 50–121 AD): Chinese eunuch credited with inventing paper, which revolutionized the way books, scrolls, and other written documents were produced.

Mani (216–c. 274 AD): Mani, a Persian prophet, was also an entrepreneur who traveled extensively throughout the Roman Empire, trading in goods like silk and spices.

Aryabhata (476–550 AD): An Indian mathematician and astronomer known for his contributions to trigonometry and calculus, Aryabhata also wrote treatises on economics and trade and advised Indian merchants on matters of finance and commerce.

Khosrow I (c. 512–579 AD): A Persian king known for his military conquests and his patronage of the arts and sciences, he also implemented a number of economic reforms, built roads and canals, encouraged the development of new industries, and promoted trade with other countries.

Harsha (590–647 AD): An Indian emperor during the seventh century AD, Harsha was known for his patronage of the arts and sciences, and encouraging the development of new industries like textiles and handicrafts. He also built a vast network of roads and canals that helped to facilitate trade and commerce throughout his empire.

Empress Wu Zetian (624–705 AD): Chinese empress during the Tang dynasty known for her intelligence, political

acumen, and entrepreneurial spirit. Her economic reforms stimulated trade and commerce and encouraged the development of new industries like textiles and ceramics.

And so many others whose names we'll never know risked everything to blaze new trails. Crazy or not, dirty or sanitized, they have significant impact on our civilization.

What does that mean to you?

Impactful changes in the world come from business, and every business starts with an entrepreneur. This is such a well-documented effect that Tom Loveland, founder of data and software consultancy Mind Over Machines, reminded me of journalist Fareed Zakaria's book *The Post-American World*.[21] In the book, Fareed dissects the wider societal, geopolitical, and economic impact of entrepreneurs. The strong US economy provides the foundation for a lot of things some take for granted, like a sizable military and extraordinary freedoms for its citizens.

But what drives the largest portion of the US economy?

Small- to medium-size businesses (in other words, entrepreneurs). Tom posited an interesting thought: "You could even make a case for entrepreneurship being patriotic."

I see the point. When businesses move beyond their countries of origin, many analysts find hunger in those new countries diminishing, health improving, education advancing, and wars ending. And why not? We don't like going to war against people making stuff for us, or customers buying from us. Studies like the IMF's observation on "Global Trade Liberalization and the Developing Countries" offer further validation on this. We'll probably never go to war with Vietnam again. Or with Tokyo. Or Berlin. Hopefully future trade with Beijing and Moscow will become so strong that current wars will be untenable, and future wars ridiculous.

So you, entrepreneur, serve a greater purpose. Move the

civilization forward. Strike out and explore strange new worlds and ideas. Take your risks and remember to always win by losing powerfully.

To help, here's what you do next:

STEP #1: ACCEPT YOUR ROLE

It's now your turn. Take your place alongside those who dared to sail beyond safe shores into dark waters, challenge the status quo, blast off to new planets, build the unbuildable, or climb to seemingly insurmountable heights. That means never forget:

When you find yourself in those moments of suffering and sacrifice, remember the impact your actions have had on the world, and will have in the coming ages.

When you're struggling to recover as you lose powerfully, remember: Where would the world be if entrepreneurs did not get back up?

When you hesitate leaving port for new challenges, remember: What would happen to civilization if we all started fearing change?

STEP #2: DON'T TAKE IT PERSONALLY

Yes, you employed the wrong hires, developed the failed strategy, took the risks, and made mistakes. But you knew the job was dangerous when you accepted it. That's what entrepreneurs do.

I know it's hard not to take it personally. But instead of putting it all on your back and feeling alone, try this:

Create and use a board of trusted advisers. These could be industry executives, academic experts, customers, or suppliers.

Join a fellow entrepreneur group.
Engage your employees.

It's easy to think that you're alone, but you're not. Share your burdens. When faced with problems, it's amazing how people rally around you when you let them. Great teams lock arms and go into battle together. It's all part of the game of entrepreneurship.

By focusing more brains on your problems, you can reach better solutions, and faster.

Ben Horowitz experienced exactly this. "When I ran Opsware and we were losing too many competitive deals, I called an all-hands and told the whole company that we were getting our asses kicked, and if we didn't stop the bleeding, we were going to die. Nobody blinked. The team rallied, built a winning product, and saved my sorry ass."

That's how you do it. It's not personal, and the journey is never easy. That's why only a few change the world.

STEP #3: GIVE BACK TO OTHERS CLIMBING BEHIND YOU

Winning isn't the end. When you succeed and have the life you dreamed of, don't forget your responsibility to teach others. "Send the elevator back down."[22] Like Mark Panciera says, "Most of us want to contribute to the world, and not just sit here, taking up space. The generation of people coming into the workforce today are looking for organizations that have a purpose beyond just making money, and many of them may decide to make their own mark through becoming entrepreneurs themselves. The idea is that if they are their own boss, then they can ensure that they and their businesses are

making a positive difference in the world. They may not be able to change the entire world, but they can change their corner of it."

So, new entrepreneurs need your help. Find one. There are plenty around. Find out what they need. Your advice, or a financial kick, or just a shoulder to lean on? Some may need an introduction to a customer, a connection with a supplier, or a skill to learn. Doesn't matter. Reach out and help.

And when you see someone hitting an EWOD, scared and uncertain, show them how to win and, more importantly, how to lose powerfully.

STEP #4: GIVE BACK TO THE VILLAGE

> "How you decide to live and be in the world will reflect outwardly in your actions, but only you will know your true spirit of intent."
>
> —Lou Tice

Extend your entrepreneurial impact beyond your customers and into the towns and cities that need your advice, products, or services. An example of this happened in 1988, years before Irish peace accords were signed. Derry, a city in Northern Ireland, reached out to Lou Tice to speak on a film being produced for that area. In the BBC studio where they shot the film, the audience consisted of warring factions of the Troubles, the ethnonationalist conflict in Northern Ireland that lasted from the late 1960s to 1998. Prior to starting, Lou went outside for a bit of fresh air. A BBC cameraman was there having a smoke. He looked at Lou and said, "Do you know who you have in there? You'll be fucking lucky if you get out alive!"

Lou went back into the studio in front of a group several

hundred Derry citizens. He knew the city was desperate for help. He asked, "What kind of Derry do you want?" He was met with stunned silence. "I don't think the citizenry of Derry had ever pondered their ability to take charge of their own and their city's futures."

Seeing the need, Lou recommended that the citizens shift their beliefs. But they needed help. So, The Pacific Institute (TPI) offered them the Investment in Excellence curriculum that had already been used by millions around the world.

What was this entrepreneur's transformational impact on Northern Ireland?

He expected a few hundred would participate. Surprisingly, one-third of the population, about thirty-four thousand citizens, chose to go through the program! The push to change Derry was launched.

Lou created another entrepreneurial miracle in South Los Angeles, with the A Better LA project. Back then, kids were killing kids—it was so common that the newspaper stories of four or more kids killed overnight were buried on page eight. Gangs had taken over the public parks, and parents didn't dare let their kids out of the house. Seeing the possibility for change, TPI worked with USC coach Pete Carroll and engaged multiple TPI clients, agencies, and school administrators. Together with the city government and parks department, the Saturday Night Lights project was born. Citizens focused on cleaning and restoring four parks, inviting the neighborhoods to return. Those four parks eventually became eight, and it multiplied from there. Slowly the parks became the neighborhood resources they were meant to be.

But the job wasn't over.

TPI went to the schools and neighborhood centers to put teens through one of their personal development courses. The result? Feedback from the teens that said, "My future was

either jail or the grave. This gave me hope for a different future." The transformation was occurring. Gang violence receded, and the killings nearly disappeared.

Your helping others through the valley of the shadow ensures more of us reach the other side. Remember, you are the driving force behind the evolution of civilization.

Give back.

THE END OF THE BEGINNING

Thanks for hanging in there and spending time with me. You made it through the labyrinth of diverse scientific areas, ancient history, and modern management findings. By dispelling a few myths and understanding the hidden secret for losing powerfully, you're now ready to engage a new phase for your entrepreneurial enterprise. And ready to help others on the journey.

Over the years of developing this material, many entrepreneurs who are now successful CEOs said they wished they had had this book earlier. I had about a dozen over to my house to review the manuscript. One CEO said, "This is the first time a book showed what real entrepreneurship looks like. I actually had my family read it so they knew what I went through!" Another CEO said, "I'm going to keep a dozen copies on the shelf so I can hand it out the next time an employee says they want to leave and start their own company. They have no idea what it's really like." Others said they'll distribute this book inside their companies to encourage and prepare employees for intrapreneurship.

I appreciate all their feedback, but I'm more interested in you. If you're thinking of launching a venture, hopefully this prepares you for the risk and suffering you'll probably experience to achieve future success. If you already started and are hitting an Entrepreneur Wall of Despair (EWOD), hopefully it gives you what you need to move past it.

This book ending launches you on a new beginning.

Now share what you learned. You run into dozens of entrepreneurs or intrapreneurs every day. Tell them about any helpful insights you gained from this book and spread the word.

Stay committed. Win and lose powerfully. Change the world.

If interested in keynote speeches, executive workshops, The Pacific Institute's training programs, or to download Don's "Mythbusting" PDF, visit www.SagaLeadership.com.

ACKNOWLEDGMENTS

I created this book standing on the shoulders of some brilliant minds, including many colleagues in the field and over thirty thousand CEOs in my workshops. The insights evolved rapidly over the years with expeditions to remote regions, support from various universities, and many ancient texts.

The colleagues I feel especially grateful for are: Cy Wakeman (*New York Times* bestselling author) for helping me see reality differently and gain more confidence in the path, George Stalk (creator of the breakthrough notion of "time-based competition" and other leading ideas in his numerous *Harvard Business Review* articles) for our brain-meld sessions on so many diverse topics on civilization and leadership, Dr. David Buss (founder of evolutionary psychology) for providing a deeper platform for understanding our species, and Dr. Cathy Trower (taking on the Governance as Leadership concept at Harvard and beyond) for jumping in with me years ago as we launched the early stages of this at Johns Hopkins.

Two associations have been particularly helpful in the development of the research for this book. First, I want to thank Vistage/TEC and its members for allowing me to validate the application of this research with thousands of CEOs in over 1,500 speeches globally for more than thirty years. Second, I want to acknowledge the National Speakers Association (NSA) and its support for me and thousands of speakers and authors. I especially want to thank all my advisers in the NSA "Million Dollar Speakers Group," particularly Jeffrey Hayzlett,

David Newman, Michelle Villalobos, Joel Block, Bill Cates, Ford Saeks, Shep Hyken, Verne Harnish, and Verl Workman for graciously spending time exploring ideas and guiding me on my ever-evolving business strategy.

A special shoutout to Mark Levy, who helped Simon Sinek find his "why," for helping me find mine; Dov Baron (*Inc.* Magazine Top 100 Leadership Speaker) for uncovering my mythbusting capacity; and Marx Acosta-Rubio (Inc. 500 CEO) for inspiring me with concepts and many of the case studies used in this book.

Field-testing these concepts in our strategic planning and executive development retreats in over one hundred industries wouldn't be possible if I didn't have colleagues to support me. Thank you, Susan Barrett, as we logged millions of miles for thirty years of sleep-deprived trips in so many cities. And thanks to Susan Rothman for recently working retreats with me and inspiring a more powerful business model. I also want to thank Bill Clark and his CEO members of Clark Leadership for being very helpful in the early stages of this book by reviewing and providing much-needed feedback.

Organizing and keeping my sanity would not be possible without my personal assistant, Stacy Adams, who keeps the office running and my calendar logistics clear in the wake of my life of constant chaos.

Finally, I want to thank my developmental editor, Rachel K, and the excellent publishing team at Girl Friday. The marketing success of this book is due in no small part to Reshma Kooner, Laura Dailey, Georgie Hockett, and Paul Barrett.

WHAT IS THE PACIFIC INSTITUTE?

For over fifty years The Pacific Institute (TPI) has taken the very scientific language of leading cognitive psychologists and social learning theorists and translated it into easy-to-understand, everyday, commonsense concepts and principles. The institute now provides courses on how the human mind works—how we think, why we think the way we do—and a structured process to change all of these learned thoughts and actions to get where we want to go, removing the biggest obstacle to our own success—ourselves.

Institute programs have been used by half the Fortune 1000 and thousands of small companies and governments in every industry, including the industry of education itself. Over seven million students in over sixty countries have participated in these programs.

I am honored to be included as part of their team.

NOTES

1. Jessica Glazer, "ADHD Can Be a CEO's Secret Superpower," *HuffPost*, September 13, 2015. Updated September 13, 2016. https://www.huffpost.com/archive/ca/entry/adhd-can-be-a-ceos-secret-superpower_b_8124154.
2. Russell Eisenstat, Bert Spector, Michael Beer, "Why Change Programs Don't Produce Change," *Harvard Business Review*, Nov.–Dec. 1990 issue.
3. *Fortune* Global 500 list in May 2022.
4. Mark Manson, *The Subtle Art of Not Giving a F*ck: A Counterintuitive Approach to Living a Good Life* (New York: HarperCollins, 2016), p. 150.
5. Geoffrey Nunberg, "Do jerks make better leaders?," *Washington Post*, September 7, 2012.
6. For a downloadable copy of Seth's new book, *Market Domination for Podcasting*, and access to live training sessions on his secret sauce, visit www.ultimatemarketingmagician.com.
7. Will Henshall was in the London Beat, a UK pop-soul band with two number-one singles in the USA, from 1991 to 1994. He was also BMI-PRS songwriter of the year 1991 for "I've Been Thinking of You."
8. Ray Kurzweil is a world-leading inventor, thinker, and futurist. Described as "the restless genius" by the *Wall Street Journal* and "the ultimate thinking machine" by *Forbes* magazine, Ray was selected as one of the top entrepreneurs by *Inc.* magazine, which described him as the "rightful heir to Thomas Edison."

PBS selected him as one of the "sixteen revolutionaries who made America." Ray holds twenty-one honorary doctorates and honors from three US presidents.

9. Stephen Evans, "Korea's hidden problem: Suicidal defectors," BBC News, November 5, 2015.
10. Nick Anderson, "SAT scores at lowest level in 10 years, fueling worries about high schools," *Washington Post*, September 3, 2015. https://www.washingtonpost.com/local/education/sat-scores-at-lowest-level-in-10-years-fueling-worries-about-high-schools/2015/09/02/6b73ec66-5190-11e5-9812-92d5948a40f8_story.html.
11. W. Keith Campbell, PhD, professor of psychology at the University of Georgia, is the author of more than two hundred papers and several books, including the latest, *The New Science of Narcissism*. Dr. Campbell has appeared in most major media outlets, including the *Today* show.
12. R. Albert Mohler, Jr., "The Self-Esteem Movement Backfires—When Praise Is Dangerous," https://albertmohler.com/2007/02/16/the-self-esteem-movement-backfires-when-praise-is-dangerous.
13. R. Albert Mohler, Jr., "The Self-Esteem Movement Backfires—When Praise Is Dangerous," https://albertmohler.com/2007/02/16/the-self-esteem-movement-backfires-when-praise-is-dangerous.
14. Carol Dweck, "The Perils and Promises of Praise," *Educational Leadership*, October 2007 (Vol. 65, No. 2, p. 34–39).
15. R. Albert Mohler, Jr., "The Self-Esteem Movement Backfires—When Praise Is Dangerous," https://albertmohler.com/2007/02/16/the-self-esteem-movement-backfires-when-praise-is-dangerous.
16. Will Storr, "'It was quasi-religious': the great self-esteem con," *Guardian*, June 3, 2017. https://www.theguardian.com/lifeandstyle/2017/jun/03/quasi-religious-great-self-esteem-con.

17. Dilvin Yasa, "Has the self-esteem movement failed our kids?," *Child* magazine, September 22, 2014. https://www.childmags.com.au/has-the-self-esteem-movement-failed-our-kids/.
18. Lauren Slater, "The Trouble With Self-Esteem," *New York Times*, February 3, 2002, Section 6, p. 44. https://www.nytimes.com/2002/02/03/magazine/the-trouble-with-self-esteem.html.
19. Ben Horowitz, "The Struggle," TechCrunch, June 14, 2012, https://techcrunch.com/2012/06/14/the-struggle/. Horowitz is now cofounder and general partner at the venture capital firm Andreessen Horowitz.
20. Charles Fishman, "No Satisfaction at Toyota," *Fast Company*, December 1, 2006.
21. Fareed Zakaria, *The Post-American World* (New York: W. W. Norton & Company, 2008).
22. A quote attributed to Édith Piaf, singer noted as France's national chanteuse and one of the country's most widely known international stars.

ABOUT THE AUTHOR

Don Schmincke is an award-winning keynote speaker, researcher, explorer, and adviser to thousands of entrepreneurs and CEOs in over one hundred industries. He began his career as a scientist doing orbital-satellite research at the Applied Physics Laboratory and then studied planetary physics, computer science, and biomedical engineering at MIT. Eventually, his interests shifted into studying humans—and all their curious behaviors. Schmincke then left MIT to begin graduate work and teaching at Johns Hopkins University, where his fascination grew into the study of how humans group for work, play, reproduction, civilization, and war. His research on humanity eventually led Schmincke on many global expeditions, visiting remote areas and regions of high conflict and connecting with brilliant scientists in different fields. During his travels he was nearly arrested as a capitalist spy in the Soviet Bloc, was launched off an aircraft carrier, survived in the Kurdish capital as Iran held US hostages, became the first white person to visit an African Tsonga village, explored religious integration in Vietnamese mountain tribes, developed missile-guidance systems while his frat brothers took Vegas (later portrayed in the movie *21*), and was caught taking his kids to a North Korean DMZ minefield. (Bad dad!)

His work has been published in over twelve languages, and he's been recommended by top business schools and has been featured by CNN, the *Wall Street Journal*, and *USA Today*. He's been named a Top 10 speaker by the largest CEO

organization and has achieved senior member recognition by IEEE, the world's largest organization for the advancement of technology.

Currently, Schmincke shares his research and strategic methods in keynote speeches, workshops, corporate events, and training sessions for CEOs across the world. He has presented at over two thousand events across five continents and has been awarded the Millennium Award and the Top Performer Award from the largest CEO organizations in the world. Today, Don flies two hundred thousand miles annually to help industries including health care, manufacturing, nonprofits, technology, finance, insurance, and the Department of Defense (where he helped the US Navy evolve its Fleet Readiness strategy), and he can occasionally be found at universities inflicting his unconventional techniques on innocent graduate students.

Schmincke is also the bestselling author of *The Code of the Executive* and *Unleash Your Potential* (a ChatGPT experiment), and the coauthor of *High Altitude Leadership.* For more information, visit www.sagaleadership.com.

OTHER BOOKS BY THIS AUTHOR

The Code of the Executive: Forty-Seven Ancient Samurai Principles Essential for Twenty-First Century Leadership Success

More than a thousand years ago, a group of business executives developed a set of principles for organizational leadership in a competitive market. Those executives were the samurai of ninth-century Japan, and their rigid code of ethics was one of the most effective frameworks for management in history.

The Code of the Executive is a modern interpretation of ancient wisdom written for today's corporate warriors. These principles provide a dynamic system of practical and moral training for effective leadership. In addition to interactive strategies for relating to the business world, this philosophy provides at its core a guide to the inner development necessary for consistent and long-term success.

High Altitude Leadership: What the World's Most Forbidding Peaks Teach Us About Success

Coauthored with Chris Warner

Leadership is often a risky, lonely role possessing nearly unbearable lows and fleeting highs. Despite this emotionally and intellectually draining roller coaster, a handful of leaders

deliver stunning results, with great consistency. They push past current leadership trends in order to achieve the most extremely challenging goals. They don't fall prey to the platitudes or cliches we see so often see in leadership theory. Instead, they succeed by recognizing and surviving the dangers that challenge them as they take themselves and their teams to higher levels.

In *High Altitude Leadership,* they show how to become that kind of leader. The authors present a new approach to leadership development based on groundbreaking scientific research, field-tested under the most brutal conditions on the most difficult summits, and successfully applied in the training of executives, management teams, and entrepreneurs throughout the world.

Unleash Your Potential: How Artificial Intelligence Wants To Upgrade YOU!

The first book of its kind. After training over thirty thousand CEOs on executive development, explorer, scientist, and best-selling author Don Schmincke decides to conduct an unusual experiment:

How would artificial intelligence train us to improve ourselves?

Don says, "I've written books and done over two thousand speeches on leadership development, so I didn't need to take on another literary project. My intention was to experiment with how AI would respond to a human request for 'personal development.'"

Don used a chatbot born in November 2022 called ChatGPT (Chat Generative Pretrained Transformer). Built on top of OpenAI's GPT-3 family of large language models, it was fine-tuned with transfer-learning and deep-learning

architectures. It then fed on what humans had published on the internet including Wikipedia, Twitter, Reddit, books, articles, web texts, and any other data scraped from all corners of the web, about three hundred billion words.

The chatbot accessed everything published, answered all of Don's questions, and wrote the book . . . all in less than two hours.

The results were surprising.

Made in United States
Orlando, FL
29 November 2023

CPSIA information can be obtained at www.ICGtesting.com
Printed in the USA
BVOW08s0239260814

364276BV00005B/20/P